ASHMOLEAN HANDBOOKS

The Arundel and Pomfret Marbles

in Oxford

MICHAEL VICKERS

2006

ISBN 1 85444 207 4 (paperback)
ISBN 1 85444 208 2 (papercased)

Titles in this series include:
Ruskin's drawings
Worcester porcelain
Maiolica
Drawings by Michelangelo and Raphael
Oxford and the Pre-Raphaelites
Islamic ceramics
Indian paintings from Oxford collections
Camille Pissarro and his family
Eighteenth-century French porcelain
Miniatures
Samuel Palmer
Twentieth century paintings
Ancient Greek pottery
English Delftware
J.M.W. Turner
Glass of four millennia
Finger rings
Frames and framing
French drawings and watercolours
Scythian and Thracian antiquities

British Library Cataloguing in Publication Data
A catalogue record for this book is available from the British Library

Cover illustration: *The sculpture gallery in Old Schools, William Westall.*

Designed and typeset in Garamond and Frutiger by Rhian Lonergan-White, Ashmolean Museum.
Printed by Craft Print, Singapore

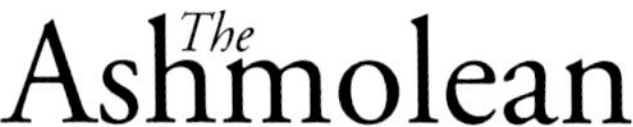

Contents

Key events

	1585	Birth of Thomas Howard
Sir Walter Raleigh's first expedition	1587	
	1595	[Saint] Philip Howard, Thomas's father, died in the Tower
Accession of James I to the throne of England on death of Elizabeth I	1603	
	1604	James I restores Thomas as Earl of Arundel, the title that had been his father's
	1606	Earl of Arundel marries Alathea Talbot, daughter of the Earl of Shrewsbury
	1613	The Earl of Arundel visits Italy with Alathea and the architect Inigo Jones
	1616	A generous gift from Lord Roos enriches the Earl of Arundel's sculpture collection
Accession of Charles I and marriage of the King to Henrietta Maria	1625	William Petty replaces John Markham as Arundel's agent
	1626	Petty acquires some two hundred inscriptions for Arundel
	1627	The collection reaches Arundel House
War with Scotland	1638	Arundel leads an embassy to the Emperor Ferdinand II in Vienna; employs Hollar; acquires gems, coins and medals from Daniel Nys' 'cabinet'.
Outbreak of English Civil War	1641	
	1642	Earl of Arundel escorts Queen and Princess Mary to Holland.

	1643	Arundel exports paintings to Holland, leaving marbles and books at Arundel House
	1645	Arundel travels to Padua
End of First Civil War	1646	Arundel dies in Padua
	1652	Henry Frederick, Arundel's heir, dies
Oliver Cromwell Lord Protector	1653	
	1654	Death of Alathea, Countess of Arundel; her son, William Lord Stafford, begins to sell the paintings
Death of Oliver Cromwell	1658	
Restoration; Charles II	1660	
	1667	Arundel House demolished. Some marbles go to Wilton House; inscriptions given to the University of Oxford
Accession of James II	1685	
William and Mary	1689	
	1692	Sir William Fermor (later Lord Leominster) buys remaining sculptures for Easton Neston
	1711	Death of Lord Leominster. His heir (later the first Earl of Pomfret) engages Guelfi to restore the sculptures
Accession of George I	1714	
Accession of George II	1727	
	1753	Death of the Earl of Pomfret; the Dowager Countess Henrietta Louisa buys sculptures from their son
	1755	Henrietta Louisa, Dowager Countess of Pomfret, presents the remaining sculptures to the University of Oxford

The Arundel and Pomfret Marbles: a brief history

Thomas Howard, the first great English art-collector (opposite) was born in 1585, the only son of Philip, Earl of Arundel. Philip, like his father the fourth Duke of Norfolk, incurred royal wrath and was imprisoned in the Tower of London where he died in 1595, never having seen his son. He was educated at home by private tutors, and as a young man 'travelled to see what they did either in Courts, as at *France* and *Rome*; or in Camps as in the *Low Countries*; or in Universities, as in *St Omers*, etc, from whence he returned a very accomplished gentleman' (Lloyd 1677, 248).

While Elizabeth was alive, Thomas's road to advancement was blocked, but with the accession of James I, he was restored to his father's title as Earl of Arundel. Many of his father's estates, however, were beyond recall, but Arundel's financial position was greatly improved when in 1606 he married Alathea, the daughter of the Earl of Shrewsbury. They immediately bought back Arundel House, the family residence that Philip Howard had inherited. The house occupied a large site by the Thames at the west end of the Strand, and had extensive gardens and courtyards.

In 1612, Arundel was unwell and was advised to travel abroad: to Spa, then Padua, where he was impressed by the charms of Italy. The next year he returned to Italy together with his wife and his friend the architect Inigo Jones. They visited in turn Venice, Padua, Florence, Siena, Rome and Naples, looking at buildings and art collections. Arundel now 'either took or improved his natural Disposition of being the great Master and Favourer of Arts, especially of Sculpture, Design, Painting and Architecture...' (Walker 1705, 212), and also began to form a sculpture collection of his own. With official permission, he excavated in the city and discovered several Roman portrait statues (see p. 14), perhaps 'planted' for his benefit (Hess 1950, 198). He enlarged his collection by commissioning the sculptor Egidio Moretti to make four colossal statues, two 'armed men' and two 'senators' (see. pp. 18–19). It was probably now that he acquired the so-called 'Homerus' (see pp. 66–67), a statue already known to Rubens (Boehringer 1939, 136–138, pls 108–13).

Back in England, Arundel was the senior representative of a family which virtually monopolised court office and official patronage, and in 1621 he was restored to the ancestral office of Earl Marshal of England. A keen interest in Holbein may be seen not simply as a link with the past, but with a past in which his own family had served with distinction and had been duly honoured. Similar, but less personal, reasons may underlie his interest in classical antiquity: it was the Roman quality of gravitas, 'a concern with order and propriety, with honour and nobility', which he seems most to have appreciated. Arundel's views were doubtless reflected in the observation of his librarian, Franciscus

Junius, that 'the arts inclined men to peace, consecrated the memory of the great, and showed virtue as the pattern of the glorious life' (Sharpe, 1978, 240; cf. Junius 1637; 1638; 1991). Arundel's personal austerity and recondite interests were well known: 'He was a man supercilious and proud, who lived always within himself and to himself... so that he seemed to live as it were in another nation, his house being a place to which all men resorted who resorted to no other place; strangers, or such who affected to look like strangers' (Clarendon 1888, 1.69).

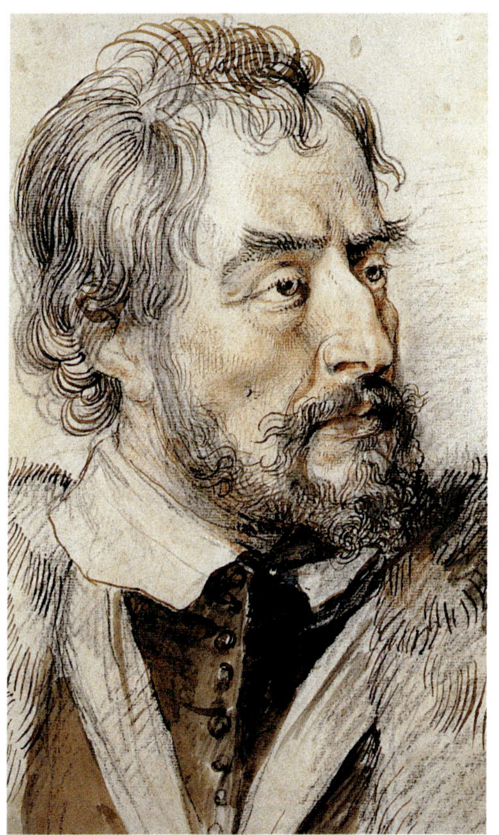

Peter Paul Rubens, *Thomas Howard, 2nd Earl of Arundel*, 1629/30

Arundel House, where members of his circle met, was being filled with paintings and sculpture acquired from Italy and western and central Europe by means of agents specially employed for the task. Details of portraits of the Earl and his Countess by Daniel Mytens (1618; see pp. 16–17) suggest that a new wing was constructed to house the collection, but the views may well be fanciful to some degree. Arundel's high position at court led to generous gifts: thus Lord Roos 'gave the Earle of Arundell all the statues he brought out of Italie at one clap', which 'exceedingly beautified his Lordship's Gallerie' (Birch 1848, 428), and at about the same time Arundel received a 'head of Jupiter' from Sir Dudley Carleton (p. 8), that was placed 'in his utmost garden, so opposite to the Gallery dores, as being open, so soon as yu enter into the front Garden yu have the head in yor eie all the way' (Hervey 1921, 101–102).

In 1621, Arundel was granted the customs dues of all the currants imported into England from the eastern Mediterranean, and was thenceforth in contact with merchants in a position to transport sculpture for him (Scott 2003, 16). In the same year, when Sir Thomas Roe was about to depart for Constantinople, Arundel asked the ambassador to collect ancient sculpture on his behalf in Greece and Asia Minor (for Roe's letters, see: Michaelis 1882,

185–204; Lapierre 2004, 462–78). Roe's efforts, however, were ineffective, and so Arundel sent out John Markham, and on the latter's death, his chaplain William Petty, to act as agents. Petty arrived in Constantinople in January 1625, at the moment when Roe had also agreed to collect antiquities for Arundel's rival, the Duke of Buckingham. Petty pretended to go along with these arrangements, which involved an attempt to remove half a dozen ancient reliefs from the Porta Aurea (at Yedi Kule), an attempt that was thwarted by rioting citizens who believed that the reliefs possessed magic properties and that the safety of the city depended on them.

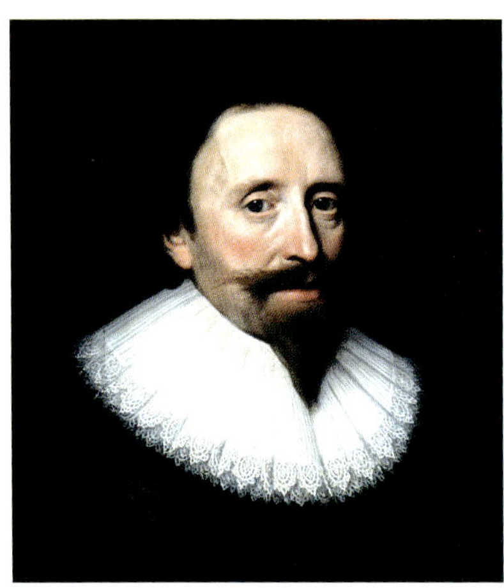

Michiel Jansz. van Mierevelt, *Sir Dudley Carleton*.

In May 1625, Petty undertook a tour of the west coast of Asia Minor, stopping first at Pergamon. Roe wrote to Buckingham in August: 'Mr Petty hathe bene at the so much famed Pergamo, and brought somewhat away, as he writes, meane things, not worth his charge, only as testimonyes of his travails; but he is a close and subtill borderer, and will not bragg of his prizes'. From there Petty went to Samos, where he acquired more sculptures; but on his return to the mainland, he was shipwrecked. The entire cargo went down with the ship. Arrested as a spy and thrown into prison, he was vouched for by Turkish friends and released and set about employing divers to recover the sunken marbles.

Roe provided new documents to enable Petty to continue his tour. Although it was clear that Petty had no intention of helping Roe supply Buckingham with antiquities, Roe had a high opinion of him, writing to Arundel: 'Ther was never a man so gifted to an imployment, that encounters all accidents with so unwearied patience; eates with Greeks on their worst dayes; lyes with fishermen on plancks, at the best; is all things to men, that he may obtayne his ends, which are your lordships service'. In Smyrna, an agent acting on behalf of the Provençal scholar de Peiresc (1580–1637), had acquired for fifty gold pieces a large number of Greek inscriptions, but was currently languishing in gaol. Petty seized the opportunity, offered a much larger sum, and secured the inscriptions – which included the chronological inscription known as the Parian Marble (see pp. 24–25) – for Arundel.

Petty spent the summer of 1626 in Athens before shipping home his acquisitions – 'two hundred pieces, all broken or few entyre', according to Roe. An essay attributed to Milton (Patterson 1938, 261) doubtless depends on experiences such as Petty's:

> The meanes to gett these things [i.e. statues] are these, there must be a passe or safe conduct from the Great Turk procured by the Ambassadour at Constantinople authorizing and securing the man employed…, to search, dig up, & transport these things only for curiosity, for the Turkes must not know that they are of any value, he that is employed must alwayes weare poor apparel, for by that meanes the Turkes will imagine the things he seeks for to be of no great estimation, he must have letters of recommendation to the English consuls, & merchants factours at every place where he goeth, with bills of exchange, & letters of credit, for the digging, carryeing, or buyeing, of the things aforesaid, he must never be without a great store of Tobacco, & English Knives, to present the Turks with all, who are governours of places, & other officers, with whome he shall have to doe; for these small presents, together with his shew of poverty, will save him from many Troubles which other wise might happen, the men that he employes to dig, he must pay by the day, and if he meet, the any Statues or Colossus's to great to be carried away whole, he must employ men to saw them asunder with Iron Sawes & sharp sand, he must use a great frame with tackles & pullies to load these on dragges or carts, he must be very carefull to gather together all the smallest bits & fragments that are found or digged up neare to any Statue, & put them up in boxes, which he must give to the masters of the ships, to be safely delivered here, he must provide Magazines or storehouses, in the port townes, which lye most convenient for his purpose, where the things are to kept, until they be transported, the best things being put in cases of boards, & th'other in the ballast, he must take heed not to load these in any ship where buts of oyle lye on the top of them, for many things have bin spoyled by that means…

The cargo arrived in London in January 1627. The new arrivals made a great stir. Arundel's friend, the libarian Sir Robert Cotton, was present at the unpacking, and, although it was the middle of the night, woke up John Selden and begged him to start work on the decipherment of the inscriptions the following morning. Selden agreed, and, with the help of Patrick Young the Royal Librarian, and Richard James the antiquary, produced *Marmora Arundeliana*, with its twenty-nine Greek inscriptions and ten Latin, before the end of 1628. It was this publication, and in particular the account of the Parian Marble, that made Arundel's name in learned Europe: de Peiresc generously stated that he was delighted to find his lost property so worthily published by his old friend John Selden.

Arundel himself weathered storms at court that were only resolved when Buckingham was assassinated in 1628. Charles I, like Buckingham, had been inspired by Arundel to collect antiquities, admitting 'a Royall liking of ancient statues, by causing a whole army of old forraine Emperors, Captaines and Senators all at once to land on his coasts, to come and doe him homage, and attend him in his palaces of St James and Sommerset House' (Peacham 1634, 107–8). Unlike Buckingham, who had been interested in works of art purely for display and required them to be complete, Arundel valued even fragments of sculpture and artists' sketches. He owned an impressive collection of the latter including hundreds of drawings by Leonardo, receiving many as a gift from the emperor Ferdinand on an embassy in 1638. It was on this journey that he took into his employment the engravers Wenceslaus Hollar and Henry van der Borcht the Younger with a view to producing a *Galleria Arundelliana* along the lines of the publications of continental collectors, and although this scheme came to nothing, the art of engraving was firmly established in England.

Henry Peacham described Arundel at the height of his renown in glowing terms:

> 'And here I cannot but with much reverence, mention the every way Right honourable Thomas Howard Lord High Marshall of England, as great for his noble Patronage of Arts and ancient learning as for his birth and place. To whose liberall charge and magnificence, this angle of the world oweth the first sight of Greeke and Romane statues, with whose admired presence he began to honour the Gardens and Galleries at Arundel-House about twentie yeares agoe, and hath ever since continued to transplant old Greece into England' (Peacham 1634, 107).

Although he laboured under heavy debts, Arundel continued to collect sculpture avidly. In 1637–8, he negotiated for the 'Statua' or 'Giulia', a 50 foot high granite obelisk that had come from Egypt in Roman times and had been used to decorate the *spina* of the Circus of Maxentius. Known as 'Mr Petty's Needle', it failed to get an export licence and it was soon to be employed by Bernini as the crowning glory of his *Fountain of the Four Rivers* (see p. 85) in Piazza Navona. As late as 1644 Arundel was prepared to pay 'any price' for the Meleager in the Palazzo Pighini in Rome (Evelyn, *Diary* November 6, 1644), and now in the Vatican (Amelung 1903–56, 2.33, No. 10); small wonder Clarendon was to state that Arundel's 'expenses were without any measure and always exceeded very much his revenue' (1888, 1.69).

The outbreak of the Civil War put an end to a last attempt at restoring Arundel's fortunes – an extravagant scheme for colonising Madagascar (portraits of the Arundels by Van Dyck show the Earl pointing at the Indian Ocean Island – see opposite). He left England never to return in 1642, and after a few years in the Low Countries, he went to Padua where he died in 1646. The only contemporary memorial is a plaque in the cloisters of the Santo in Padua recording the burial of Arundel's entrails (see p. 34).

Arundel had expressed the wish that his collection be kept together permanently (Scott 2003, 15), but this was not to be. A series of family disputes ended with Henry Howard, Arundel's grandson, taking Arundel House and its contents, and his uncle William Lord Stafford Alathea's estate, which included a bronze head known as the 'Arundel Homer', but which probably represents Sophocles (now in the British Museum: Walters 1899, No. 847). The marbles seem to have survived the Civil War,

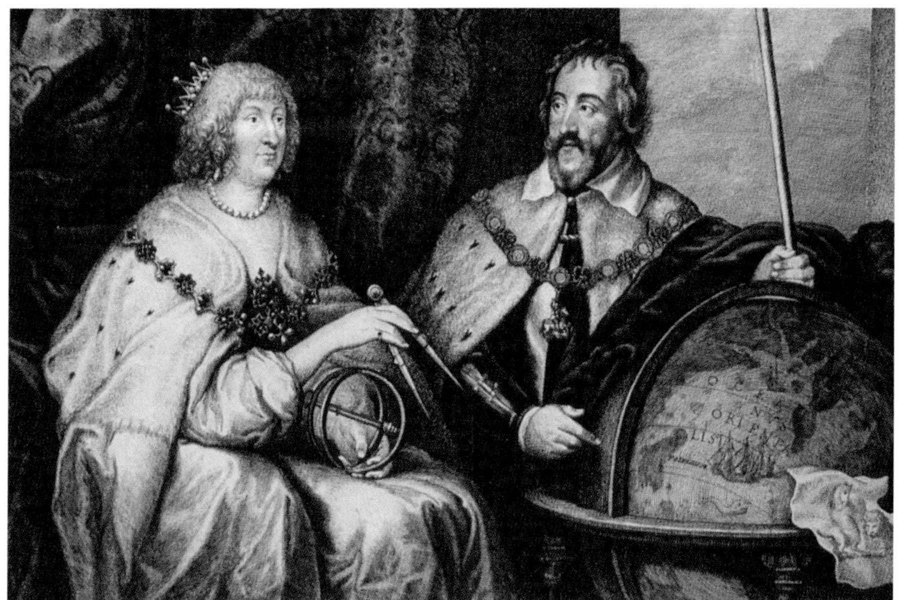

Engraving after: Anthony van Dyck, *The Madagascar Portrait*, 1639.

but suffered from vandalism. Of the two hundred and fifty inscriptions collected by Arundel one hundred and fourteen had already disappeared when in 1667 Henry was persuaded by John Evelyn to give the remainder to the University of Oxford (see p. 38). The Vice-Chancellor's accounts for 1667–68 include entries for the 'Water carriage of the Arundell Marbles' and 'for cleansing the Marbles' (Clark 1895, 69). The gift was commemorated with an inscription and the publication in 1676 of Humphrey Prideaux's *Marmora Arundelliana*. An entry in the Vice-Chancellor's accounts for 1675–76 refers to 'the *Marmora Oxoniensia*, and some other richly bound and presented to severall persons of quality' – including Elias Ashmole (p. 41), who was soon to fund the construction of the new Ashmolean Museum.

In 1677, Henry succeeded to the dukedom of Norfolk and hoped to build a new Arundel House and to decorate it with the ancient marbles still in his possession, but lost interest when he had to go ahead at the time of Titus Oates. Many busts were subsequently sold to Thomas Herbert, later eighth Earl of Pembroke, and they must be among those now at Wilton House. The rest were neglected in the grounds and some were covered with builders' rubbish, so that even though the bulk of them were eventually sold off in 1691, there were marbles still to be found on the site of Arundel House in later years (see pp. 22–23; Cook 1974). Most of the remainder were sold to Sir William Fermor for £300, some damaged pieces were given to an old family servant named Boyder Cuper who used them to furnish a pleasure ground at Lambeth, and the residue were dumped on waste ground at Kennington.

Sir William Fermor, soon to be the first Baron Leominster, took his sculpture to furnish the house and grounds at Easton Neston in Northamptonshire, and after his death in 1711, his son Thomas, later first Earl of Pomfret, had them restored at the less-than-skilled hands of Giovanni Battista Guelfi, a pupil of Camillo Rusconi (see p. 47). George Vertue visited Easton Neston around 1734 and has left a description of the way the marbles were disposed (Vertue 1758). A notable feature was a remarkable ornament known as 'The Tomb of Germanicus' (see. pp. 44–45). Many statues were exhibited in a conservatory, and described by Horace Walpole as 'a wonderful fine statue of Tully [Cicero: see p. 15] haranguing a numerous assembly of decayed emperers, vestal virgins with new noses, Colossus's, Venus's, headless carcases and carcasless heads, pieces of tombs and hieroglyphics' (Letter to G. Montague, May 20, 1736).

The glories of Easton Neston were temporary. On the first Earl of Pomfret's death, his son's debts were such that he sold the sculpture collection to his mother, the Dowager Countess Henrietta Louisa, who in turn presented it in 1755 to the University of Oxford (see pp. 52–53). Fifty-one statues, twenty-two busts and heads and thirty-nine reliefs and other sculptures came to Oxford (the 'Pomfret marbles') to rejoin the inscriptions from the Arundel collection that had been given in 1667. A lavish publication, *Marmora Oxoniensia*, by Richard Chandler appeared in 1763. Their first home was in the Old Schools (see pp. 56–57), but eventually the Pomfret marbles were transferred to Cockerell's new University Galleries, the present Ashmolean Museum.

Boyder Cuper's statues in Lambeth (in 'Cupid's Gardens') were neglected until in 1719 they were illustrated in John Aubrey's *Natural History and Antiquities of Surrey* (5.pls 1–8). Soon afterwards they were acquired for £75 by John Freeman of Fawley Court, Henley-on-Thames, and Edmund Waller of Hall Barn, Beaconsfield. Thanks to detective work by Mr and Mrs Denys Haynes in the 1960s, many of these pieces were re-discovered (Haynes 1974; 1975 [a work to which the present writer is much indebted]). An Attic altar (see p. 65) and the Arundel 'Homerus' (see p. 67) are now in the Ashmolean. A Giant from the Great Altar of Zeus at Pergamon at Fawley Court (Haynes 1972) is now in London. Some of the pieces from Kennington were eventually acquired by Lord Burlington for Chiswick House, and 'six statues, without heads or arms, lying close to each other; some of a Colossal size, the drapery of which was thought to be exceeding fine' were sent to Worksop Manor (J. Theobald in Howard 1769, 104–5), where all except one were destroyed in a fire in 1761. The survivor proved to be another Pergamene Giant (Haynes 1963), which is now in the Worksop Public Library. A column drum from

Kennington was taken to White Waltham in Berkshire, to be used as a roller for a bowling green. As Adolf Michaelis (whose account of the history of collecting in England remained unsurpassed until recently: see now Scott 2003) remarked in 1882, *sic transit gloria mundi.*

Acknowledgements

Reference has already been made to the debt owed by the author to the late Denys Haynes's *The Arundel Marbles* (Oxford, 1975). Elizabeth Angelicoussis, Christopher Brown, Cristiano Giometti, Nick Davey, Sybille Haynes, John Martin Robertson, Bettina Schmitt, David Sturdy and Susan Walker provided advice and encouragement. Ersin Hussein and Agnieszka Frankowska provided invaluable help. All illustrations here are of objects, paintings or engravings in the Ashmolean, unless otherwise stated. Thanks are due in the first instance to the Ashmolean's photographers, David Gowers and Nick Pollard, for their careful work. Design and layout were in the capable hands of Rhian Lonergan-White. Kate Heard and Declan McCarthy were instrumental in providing and obtaining illustrations from the Department of Western Art and from institutions outside the Ashmolean. Particular thanks are due to the following: the Provost and Fellows of Worcester College (for p. 14), the National Portrait Gallery (for p. 17), the Governing Body, Christ Church, Oxford (for p. 23 top), the British Library (for p. 45), the British Museum (for p. 33), to David Sturdy (for p. 41), Küpferstichkabinett, Staatliche Museen zu Berlin (for p. 67, left), the Musée du Louvre (for p. 67 below), Rendel Schlüter (for p. 74), Sybille Haynes (for p. 85). Photos on pp. 34 and 85 bottom right, are by the author.

Roman Excavations

In 1606, at the age of twenty, Arundel married Alathea, third daughter of the Earl of Shrewsbury, who brought him a considerable fortune. In 1613 they travelled abroad in the company of Inigo Jones, visiting Venice, Padua, Florence, Siena, Rome and Naples, and seeing the buildings and art collections of Italian prelates and princes. This was when, according to Sir Edmund Walker, Arundel 'either took or improved his natural Disposition of being the great Master and Favourer of Arts, especially of Sculpture, Design, Painting and Architecture...' (Clopton 1705, 212). It was in Rome that Arundel began the formation of his own collection of sculpture: 'Lord Arundel, when at Rome, procured permission to dig over the ruins of several houses, and is said to have discovered, in subterraneous rooms, ... statues, all of which are presumed to be portraits of a consular family' (Dallaway 1800, 256–7; cf. Hess 1950, 198 who implies that the statues had been 'planted' for Arundel's benefit).

One of the statues (Michaelis 45; second century AD; H.: 2.17 m; Pomfret gift) is a powerful figure wearing a toga, the head and extremities restored since antiquity; the restorer even placed a wart [*cicer*] on the right cheek in order to make him into Cicero. George Vertue was greatly impressed when he saw this statue in Easton Neston: 'Marcus Tullius Cicero, bigger than life, with his handkerchief in his right hand... 'Tis exquisitely fine; my lord [Pomfret] hath been bid three thousand pounds for this noble figure.'

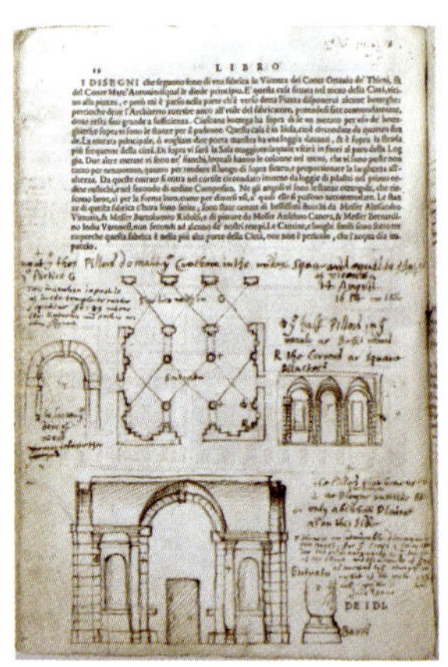

Inigo Jones's annotated copy of Andrea Palladio's *I quattro libri dell'architettura* (1601). Worcester College, Oxford.

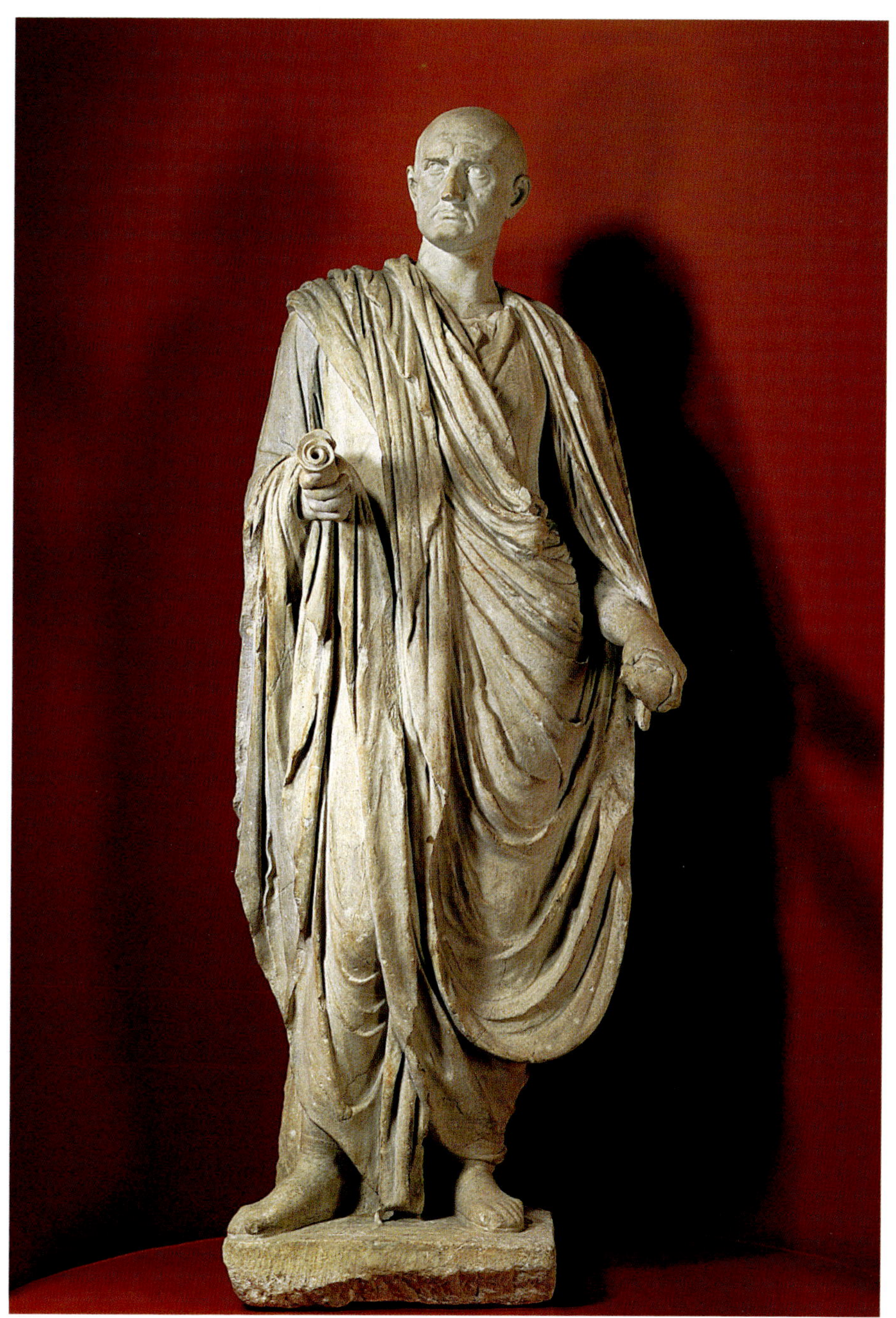

Arundel House

One of the first things Arundel did after his marriage was to buy back Arundel House, which occupied a large site on the north bank of the Thames at the east end of the Strand. Classical inscriptions were applied to the walls of the house, so that Henry Peacham could say 'You shall find all the walls of the house inlaid with them and speaking Greek and Latin to you. The garden especially will afford you the pleasure of a world of learned lectures in this kind' (1634, 124–5). Sir Francis Bacon was even more enthusiastic: 'coming into the Earl of Arundel's Garden, where there were a great number of Ancient statues of naked Men and Women,' he 'made stand, and as astonish'd cryed out: The Resurrection' (Tenison 1679, 57).

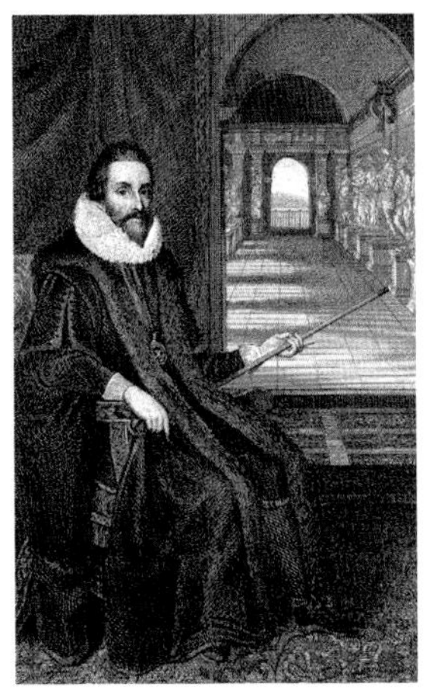

Portraits of the Earl and his Countess by Daniel Mytens show them against the background of somewhat idealized galleries, in which, however, individual works can be recognized. In the sculpture gallery, before which the Earl sits bearing his Marshal's baton, can be seen the Homerus, Bacchus, Venus, and Eros that now stand in the Ashmolean's Randolph Gallery. Alatheia Talbot was as devoted a student of the arts as her husband (Fletcher 1996). It was at her urging that their librarian Franciscus Junius's influential De pictura veterum ('The Painting of the Ancients') was translated into English in 1638 ('influential' because it was used as an unacknowledged source by Winckelmann [Junius 1991, lxxv–lxxvi]).

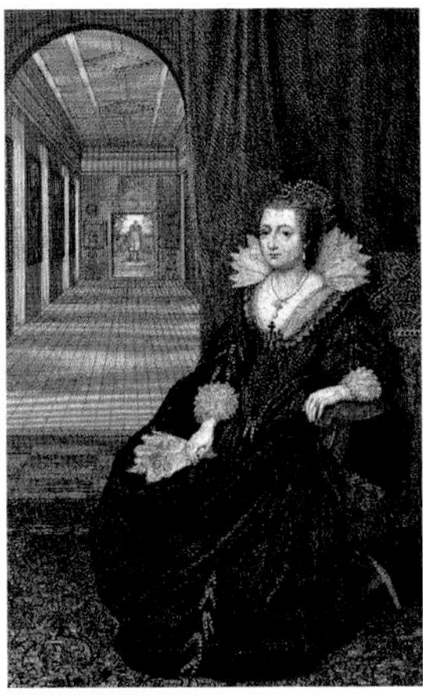

Engravings after Daniel Mytens' portraits of *Thomas Howard, 2nd Earl of Arundel* and *Alathea Talbot, Countess of Arundel*, *c.*1618.
The originals (detail opposite) are on loan to the National Portrait Gallery from Arundel Castle.

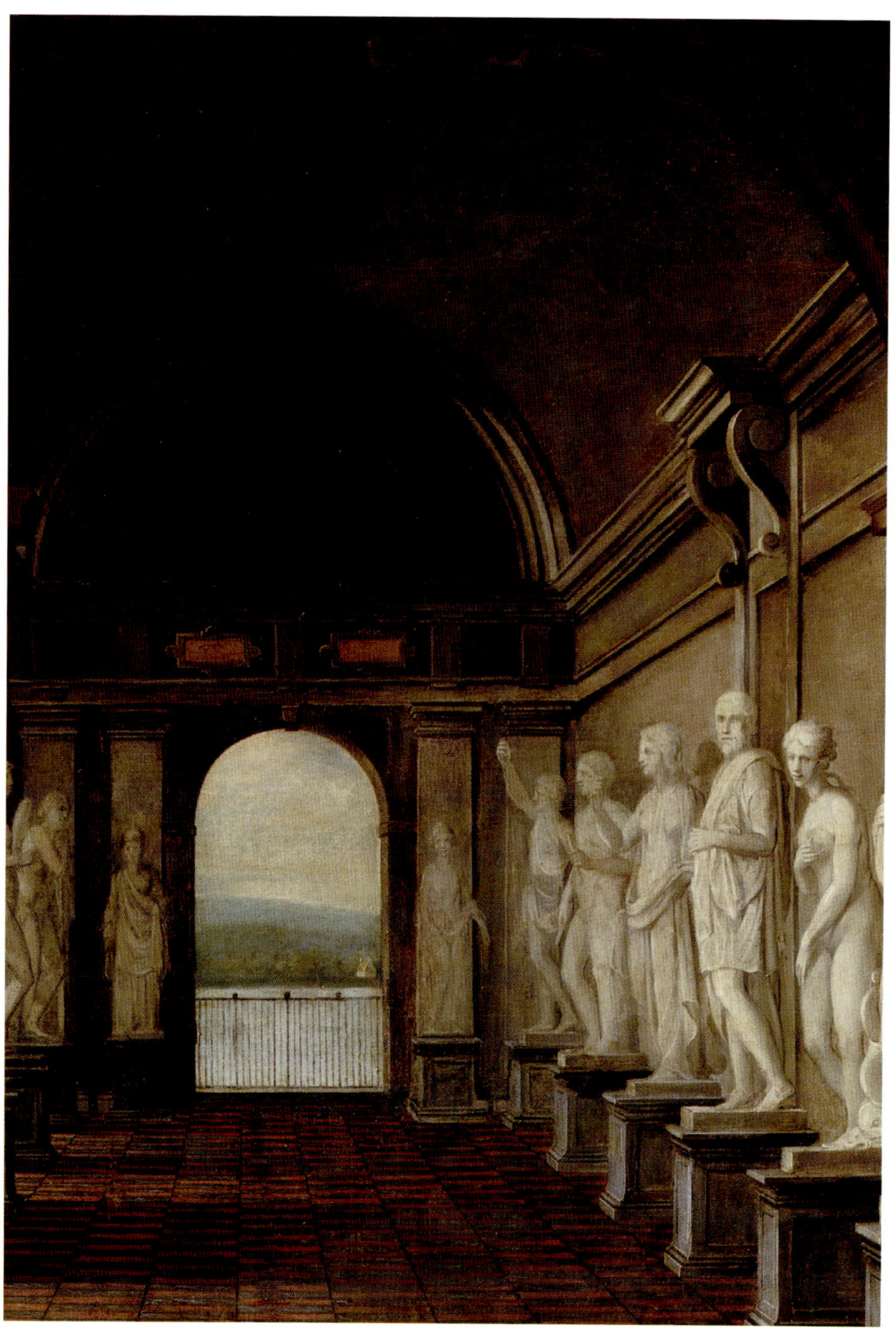

Early Patronage

A limestone bust of Henry VIII surviving amongst the marbles at Oxford (AN G. 1228; Ht. 67 cm; Pomfret gift) is a reminder of Arundel's interest in relics of the days when his family's influence had been at its height. The bust itself has a curious artistic pedigree, having been copied from an Italian marble bust belonging to his uncle Lord Lumley, which in turn was based on a medal of the king, which itself depended on a painting or drawing by Holbein (Vickers 1980; Penny 1992, No. 599).

Arundel acquired several pieces of ancient sculpture during his Roman stay, as we have seen. There was, however, a limit to the extent to which even an illustrious foreigner might be allowed to remove ancient remains. In June 1614, Arundel therefore commissioned four statues ('two senators' and 'two armed men' [Michaelis 46, H.: 2.13 m; Michaelis 47, H.: 2.165 m; AN G. 1150, H.: 2.24 m; AN G. 1151, H.: 2.165 m; Pomfret gift]) from the Roman sculptor Egidio Moretti (Vickers 1979a; Penny 1992, Nos 64–67). Moretti was not the most accomplished artist of the day; again local patrons had the first choice of the talent available, and a foreigner had to be content with what he could get. Moretti was born in Rome around 1585, and in 1613 we hear of him at work on the façade of St Peter's, where we know from account books that he was responsible for carving two statues (Hess 1950). Arundel's statues were seen by Vertue in the garden at Easton Neston in 1734: 'two fine statues of the Two Scipio's, in the general's habit, very perfect and exceeding fine'. Vertue took them (and the 'senators') as 'true antiques', but he should have noticed the Howard, Fitzalan and Talbot armorial animals (lions, horses and hounds) on the lappets of the cuirasses. These animals also occur on a pair of low table supports that may also have been made by Moretti (Michaelis 123, 124; H.: 60 cm, W.: 1.16–1.20 m; Pomfret gift; Haynes 1975, 22).

Clockwise: Anon. *Henry VIII*; Egidio Moretti, *Armed Man* (1614); ? Egidio Moretti, *Table support.*

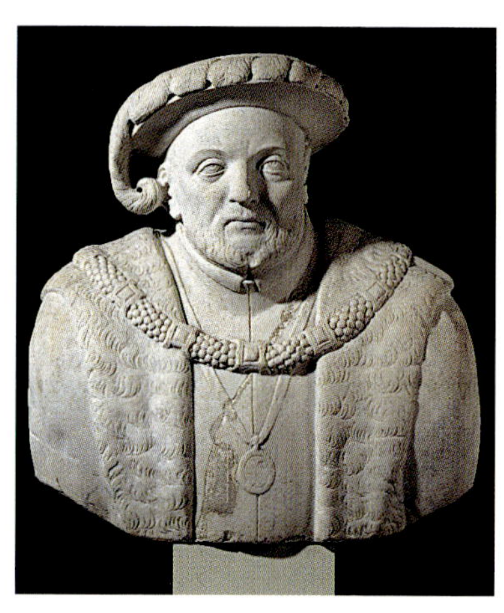

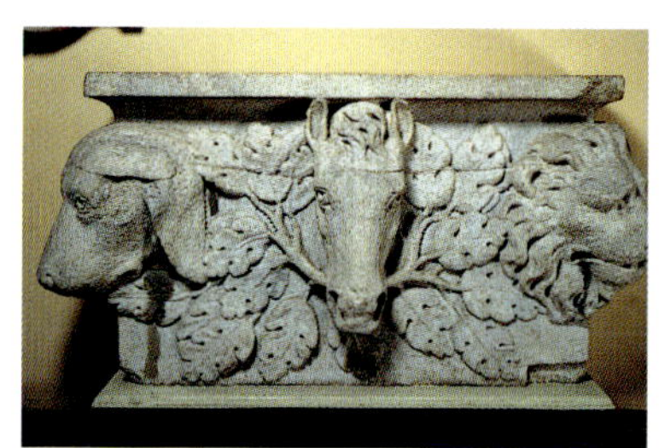

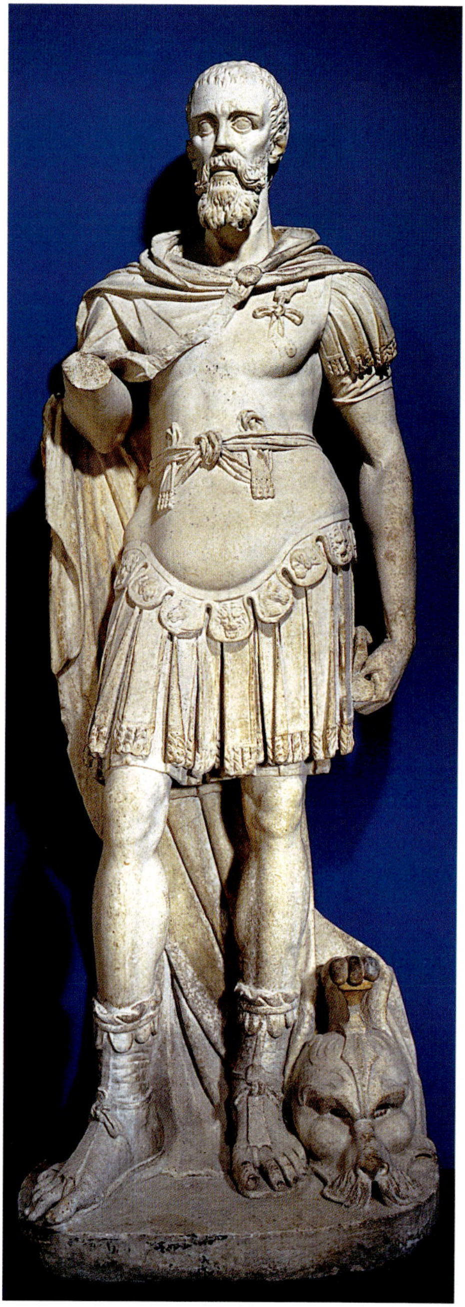

The Sack of Troy

Second century AD
28 cm x 2.11 m
Pomfret gift 1755 — Michaelis 111

This sculptured frieze comes from the lid of a Roman sarcophagus. There are three scenes, all to do with the Trojan War: on the left, the famous Wooden Horse wearing a helmet, in which the Greeks hid and which the Trojans were tricked into bringing into their beleagured city, is dragged through an arched gateway. In the centre, feasting Trojans dressed in Phrygian garments are disturbed by Greeks who attack them. On the right, an earlier event: the Greek Achilles drags the body of the Trojan hero Hector behind his chariot. The youthful heads at each end of the frieze wear Phrygian caps (Robert 1890 2, No. 64).

This fragment was known to Rubens (van der Meulen 1975, 84–5), but none of his works has as yet been associated with it. The Trojan War was extremely important both for the ideology of imperial Rome and for that of seventeenth-century European aristocracies. The Romans in general, and the imperial house in particular, reckoned their descent from the Trojan exile Aeneas. Many European noble houses included Trojan exiles among their ancestors; the Hapsburgs, for example, claimed to be in the direct line from Hector. It was a view of antiquity which was superseded during the eighteenth century when the image of the Greeks improved: no longer regarded in an invidious light, they and their culture increasingly became an inspiration for those intellectuals and politicians, largely from outside the old European aristocracies, who were seeking to establish democracies in Europe and North America.

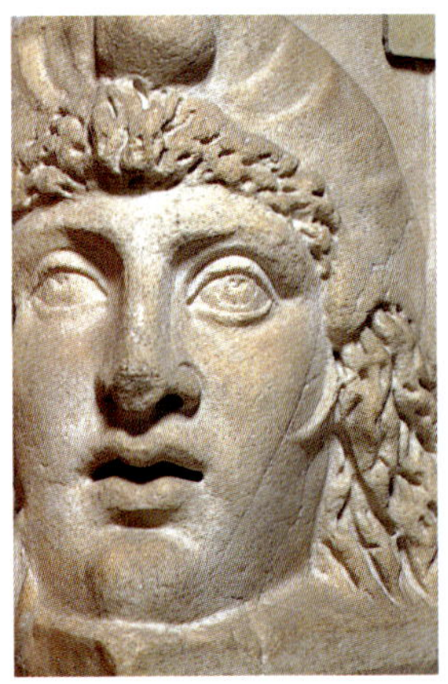

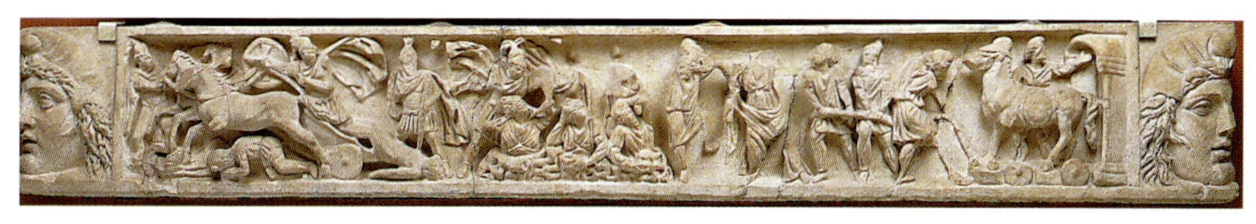

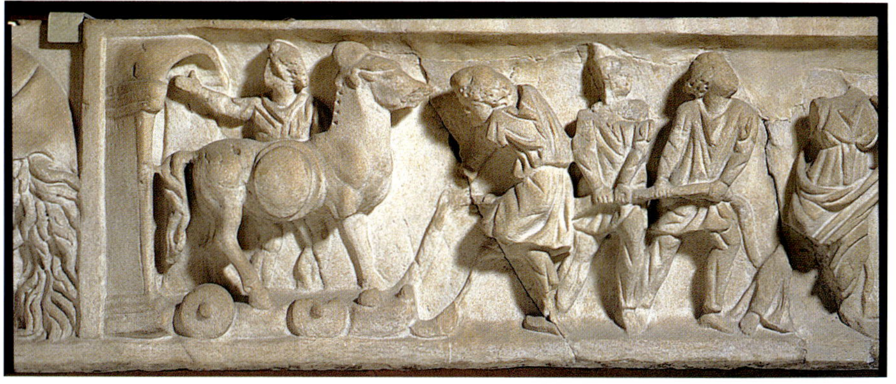

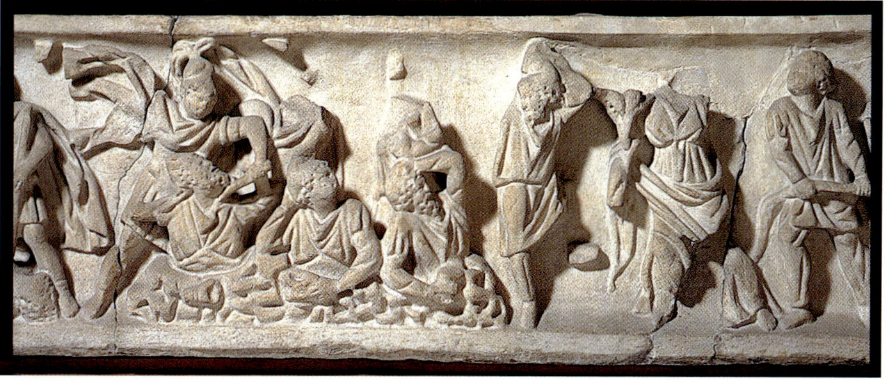

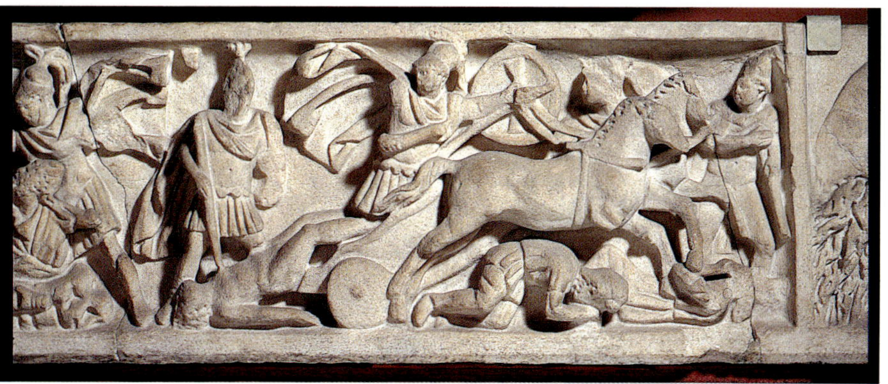

The Continence of Scipio

Excavations on the site of Arundel House in 1972 produced several fragments of ancient marble, notably a large block of bluish grey coarse-grained limestone from an architectural frieze decorated with alternating Medusa heads and consoles, now in the Museum of London (70 x 146 x 63 cm; Cook 1975). The piece was already well documented, having been drawn at Arundel House by John Webb in 1639, and it figures prominently in the foreground of Anthony van Dyck's *Continence of Scipio*, painted in late 1620 or early 1621, and now in the Christ Church Picture Gallery. The subject matter relates to Scipio Africanus's restoration of a captive slave to her betrothed, an exemplum of a victorious general's generosity and restraint.

A marginal note by Inigo Jones in his copy of Vitruvius now in Chatsworth informs us that the frieze block was acquired in Smyrna, and in view of its considerable weight it was almost certainly found locally. This will also perhaps explain why it was left behind when the rest of the sculpture was sold off in 1691.

It would be good if the presence of a substantial piece of sculpture from the Arundel collection in van Dyck's painting could throw light on patterns of patronage in Caroline England. In fact, it raises more questions than it answers. The picture belonged to the Duke of Buckingham, Arundel's rival at court and as a collector. It is even uncertain as to which of them – Arundel or Buckingham – was responsible for bringing van Dyck over from Antwerp, for during his first visit to England he is known to have painted important pictures for both noblemen. Was the Christ Church picture perhaps a gift from Arundel to Buckingham? Unlikely; more reasonable to suppose that the relief formed part of Buckingham's collection and was only acquired by Arundel after the duke's death in 1628 (White 1995).

Above: Anthony van Dyck, *Continence of Scipio*, 1620/1621, Christ Church, Oxford. Below: John Webb, *Frieze from Smyrna*, 1639.

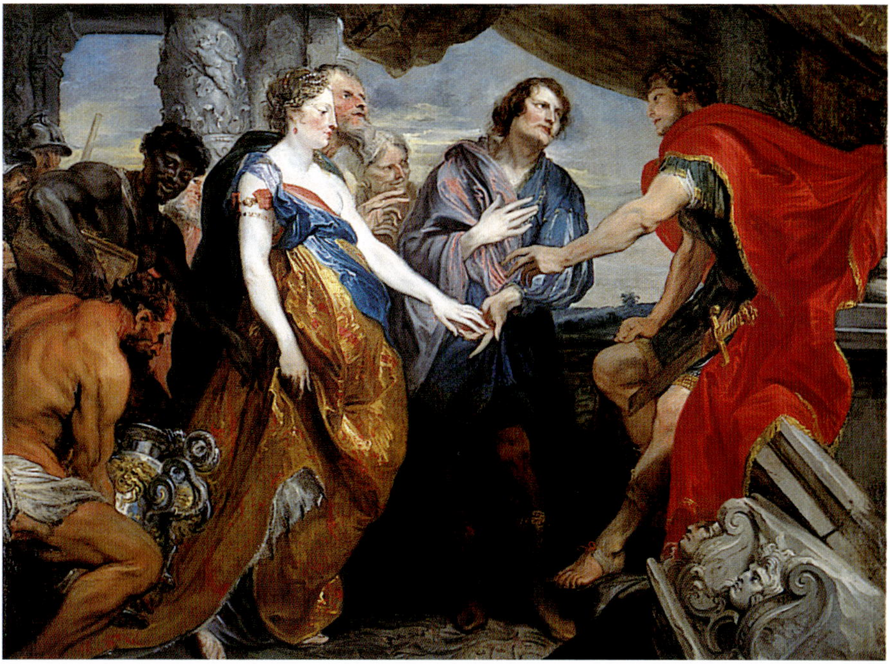

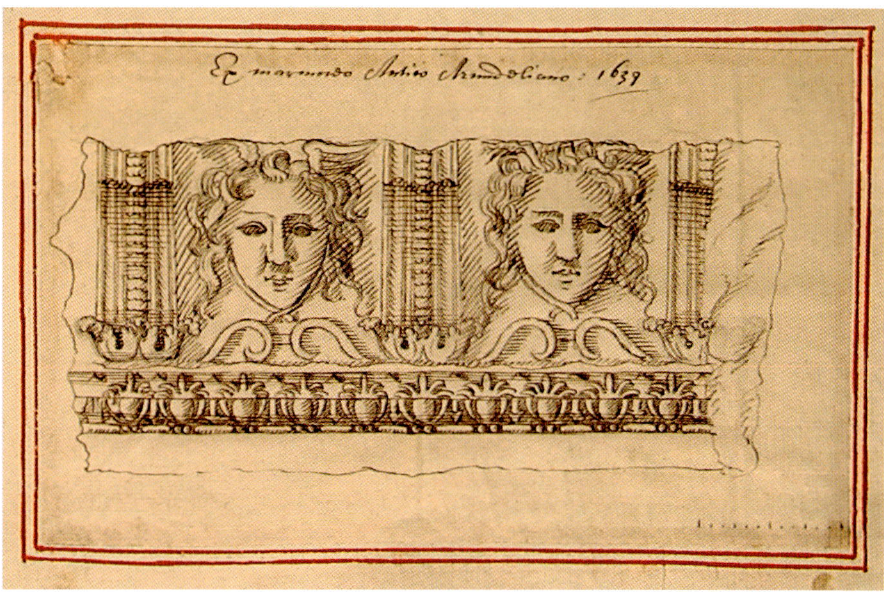
Ex marmoreo Antico Arundeliano : 1639

Parian Marble

Third century BC
H.: 56.5 cm; W.: 81.2 cm
Howard gift 1667 Chandler 2.59

The Parian Marble (otherwise known as the Parian Chronicle or the *Marmor Parium*) is the earliest extant example of a Greek chronological table (Howard gift 1667; Jacoby 1929, No. 239). The compiler's name is lost, but he covers the period from the accession of King Cecrops in Athens in, according to him, 1581/0 BC to 264/3 BC, doubtless the date of composition and of the inscription itself. For over a hundred of these thirteen hundred years, he found events to record of a very varied nature. He dates Deucalion's flood to 1528/7, the invention of corn by Demeter to 1409/8 and the fall of Troy to 1209/8. He dates Hesiod one generation earlier than Homer, in the late tenth century. As he nears his own day, his account becomes fuller, but his chronology is not always accurate and the reasons for his choice of events are not always clear. The Oxford fragment covers the years 895–355 BC.

The Parian Marble was acquired in Smyrna by Arundel's agent William Petty in 1626 from under the nose of the agent of the Provençal scholar Nicolas Claude Fabri de Peiresc, who had hoped to be the first to publish such an important document. In the event, the first study was that of John Selden, in his *Marmora Arundelliana* of 1628–9, which brought Arundel great acclaim throughout educated Europe. The top half was lost in the seventeenth century, having been used as a hearthstone. A smaller fragment, covering the years 336–299 BC, was found in Paros in 1897 and is in the museum there (see further http://www.ashmolean.org/ash/faqs/q004/).

William Petty was energetic and resourceful on Arundel's behalf. Sir Thomas Roe, the ambassador in Constantinople, observed him at work: '… I am informed hee hath gotten many things, rare, and antient. Ther was neuer man so fitted an imployment, that encounters all accident with so unwearied patience; eates with Grekes on their worst dayes; lyes with fisherman on plancks, at the best; is all things to all men, that he may obteyne his ends, which are your lordships seruice' (Lapierre, 2004).

Right: Reconstruction from *Inscriptiones Graecae*, 12.5, p.103 (No.444)

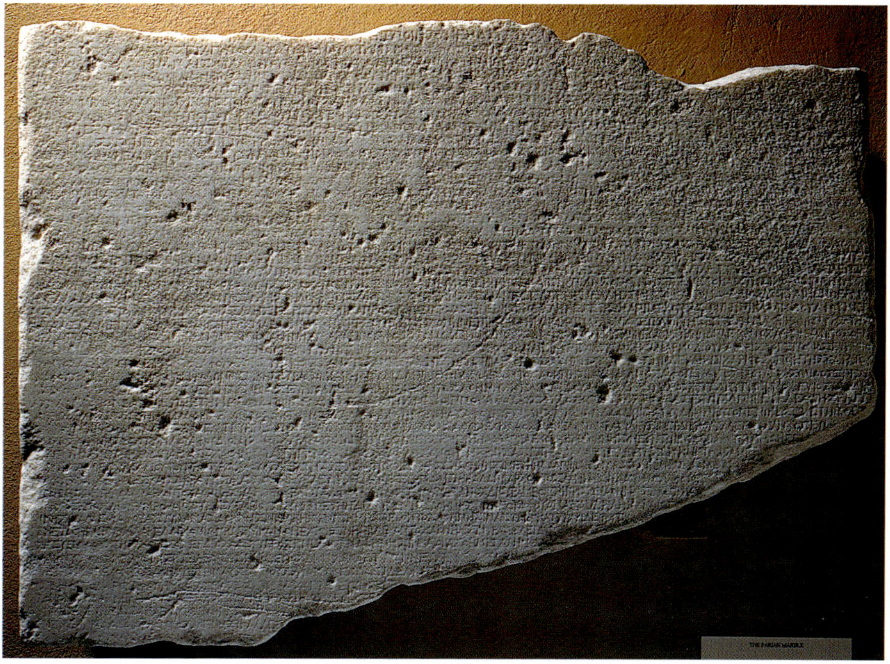

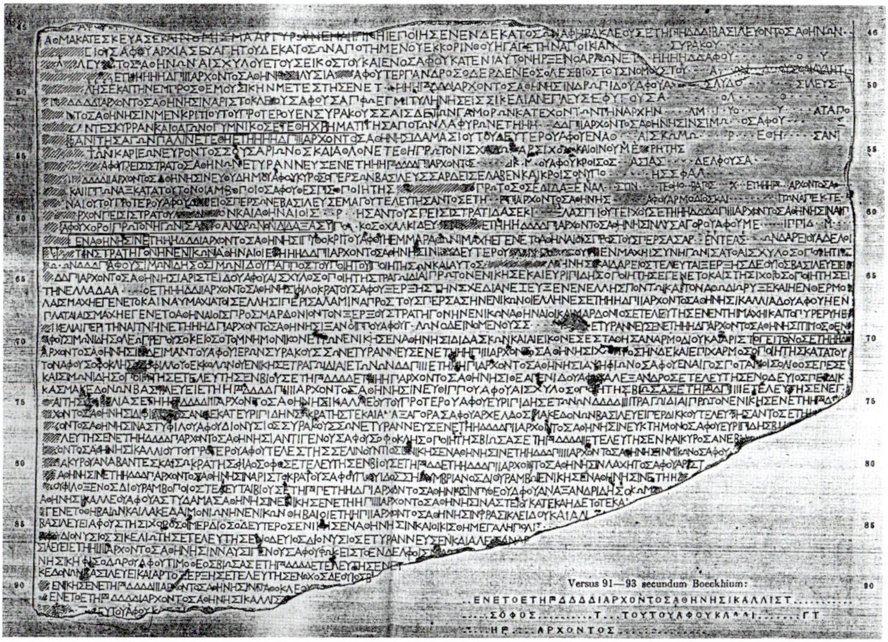

Versus 91—93 secundum Boeckhium:

..ΕΝΕΤΟΕΤΗΡΔΔΔΔΙΑΡΧΟΝΤΟΣΑΘΗΝΗΣΙΚΑΛΛΙΣΤ..........

.....ΣΟΦΟΣ..........Τ...ΤΟΥΤΟΥΑΦΟΥΚΛΑΑΙ.......ΓΤ

.....ΗΡ.....ΑΡΧΟΝΤΟΣ..........

The Felix Gem

First century AD
H.: 2.6 cm; W.: 3.5 cm
Ex-Spencer-Churchill collection 1966.1808

The Felix Gem was made for Calpurnius Severus, a member of the court of the emperor Tiberus, (AD 14–37) by the gem cutter Felix whose name is inscribed on the altar. It bears a scene of the seizure of the Palladium – an image of the goddess Pallas Athena – from the citadel at Troy. Ulysses remonstrates with his companion Diomedes for having murdered Athena's priestess, whose feet alone are visible. Neptune turns his back on the proceedings in disgust. The reference is to Rome's earliest legendary history, as told in the almost contemporary *Aeneid* of Virgil: without possession of the Palladium, the Greeks could never take Troy; and without Trojan émigrés (such as Aeneas) there would have been no Rome.

This gem formed part of the collection of Pope Paul II (1464–71), where it was considered to be the most valuable of all his intaglios, being appraised at 100 gold ducats (Dacos 1973, 103). It was probably among the objects that Cardinal Francesco Gonzaga showed to Andrea Mantegna, the Gonzaga artist in residence, in 1472, and motifs from the Felix Gem occur frequently in Mantegna's works thereafter. Vulcan in the *Parnassus* of 1497, for example, is based on both figures of the Felix Gem (Vickers 1985).

By 1637, the Felix Gem belonged to the Earl of Arundel. It is uncertain whether a cabinet of gems that the dealer Daniel Nys had been unsuccessfully trying to get Charles I to buy was that of the Gonzagas, but Arundel stepped in and acquired 263 cameos and intaglios (including the Felix Gem). William Petty accompanied the cabinet back to England. John Evelyn wrote to Samuel Pepys on 12 August 1689: 'that great lover of antiquity, Thomas, Earl of Arundel had a very rich cabinet of medals as well as other intaglias belonging to the cabinet he purchased of Daniel Nice at the cost of £10,000'. Subsequent owners of the Felix Gem include the Dukes of Marlborough (Scarisbrick 1996), Sir Arthur Evans and Captain E.G. Spencer-Churchill.

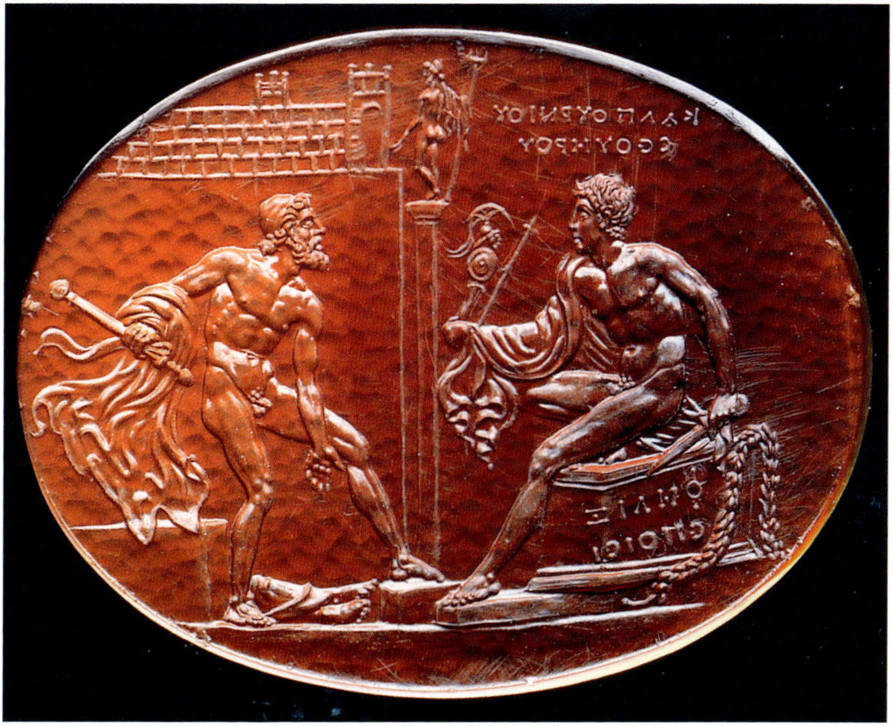

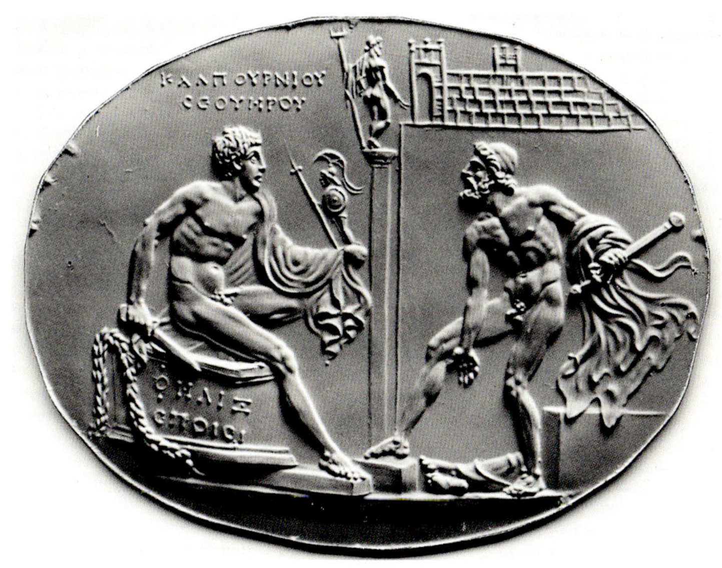
ΚΑΛΠΟΥΡΝΙΟΥ
ϹΕΟΥΗΡΟΥ
ΦΗΛΙΞ
ΕΠΟΙΕΙ

François Dieussart

François Dieussart (*c.*1600–1661) was a Flemish sculptor who had learnt his craft in Rome in the circle around Bernini, and worked for patrons in the courts of northern Europe, producing portraits in an Italianate style to a high degree of technical proficiency. He first came to England, apparently at Arundel's bidding, and made his name with the construction of a magnificent mechanical monstrance some forty feet high for Queen Henrietta Maria's chapel in Somerset House.

In the same year he made a bust of King Charles I for Arundel, and in 1637 busts of Prince Rupert of the Rhine (AN G. 1152; H.: 90.2 cm; Pomfret gift 1755; Penny 1992, No. 471) and his brother Charles Louis. Another bust of the King, now in Windsor, has all the characteristics of the Rupert bust, and is presumably a copy after Dieussart rather than Bernini, as used to be thought (Vickers 1978). Both princes were in England between 1635 and 1637, hoping to persuade their uncle, Charles I, to give his support for the restoration of the Palatinate to Charles Louis. Arundel led an unsuccessful embassy to the Emperor Rudolf in 1636 in the hopes of achieving this end.

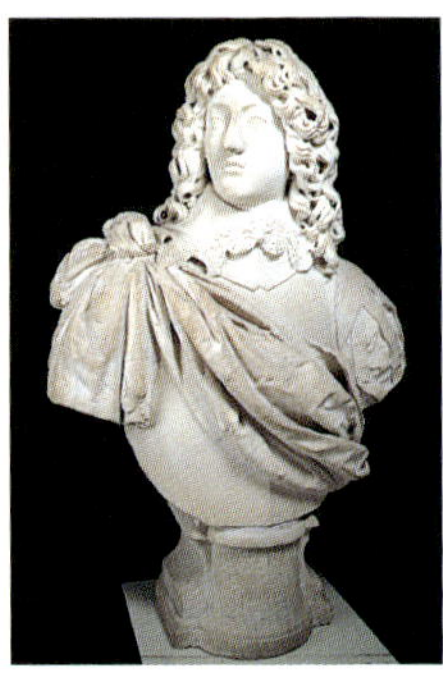

Above: François Dieussart, *Rupert of the Rhine* (1637). Right: François Dieussart, *Thomas Howard, Earl of Arundel* (1637)

The elaborate, Italianate, base of Dieussart's marble portrait of the Earl (Ht.: 1.15 m; Penny 1992, No. 472) carries the Arundel armorial animals, the lion, horse and hound. The portrait itself is as dignified, and redolent of nobility as any prince of the church by Bernini or Algardi. But what adds to its interest and importance is that it was done in England, by an artist Arundel had brought from Rome to work for him. Bernini himself had chosen not to make a sculptural portrait of Arundel and his grandson on the basis of of a painting by van Dyck.

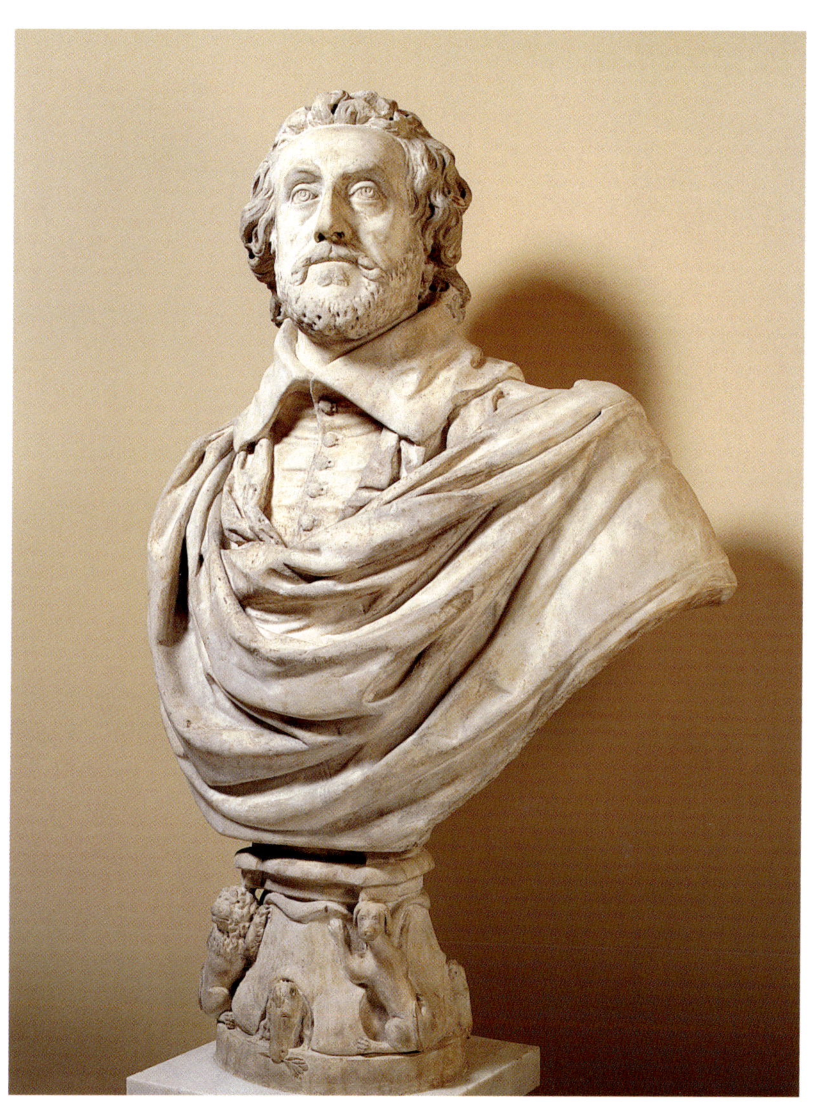

Judith and Holophernes

Seventeenth century
H.: 1.365 m
Pomfret gift 1755 | Penny 1992, No. 473

The Book of Judith, the fourth Book of the Old Testament Apocrypha relates how Judith, a widow, helped to save her home town of Bethulia in Israel when it was besieged by the army of king Nebuchadnezzar II of Babylon (*c.*604–562 BC). She enticed its general Holophernes to receive her as a guest and then beheaded him as he slept. She returned to Bethulia with the head, thus raising the spirits of her fellow-citizens and demoralising the enemy, who were then repulsed. This early seventeenth century statue made from Carrara marble, but now severely weathered, may have been carved in England by François Dieussart after a bronze statuette now in Berlin.

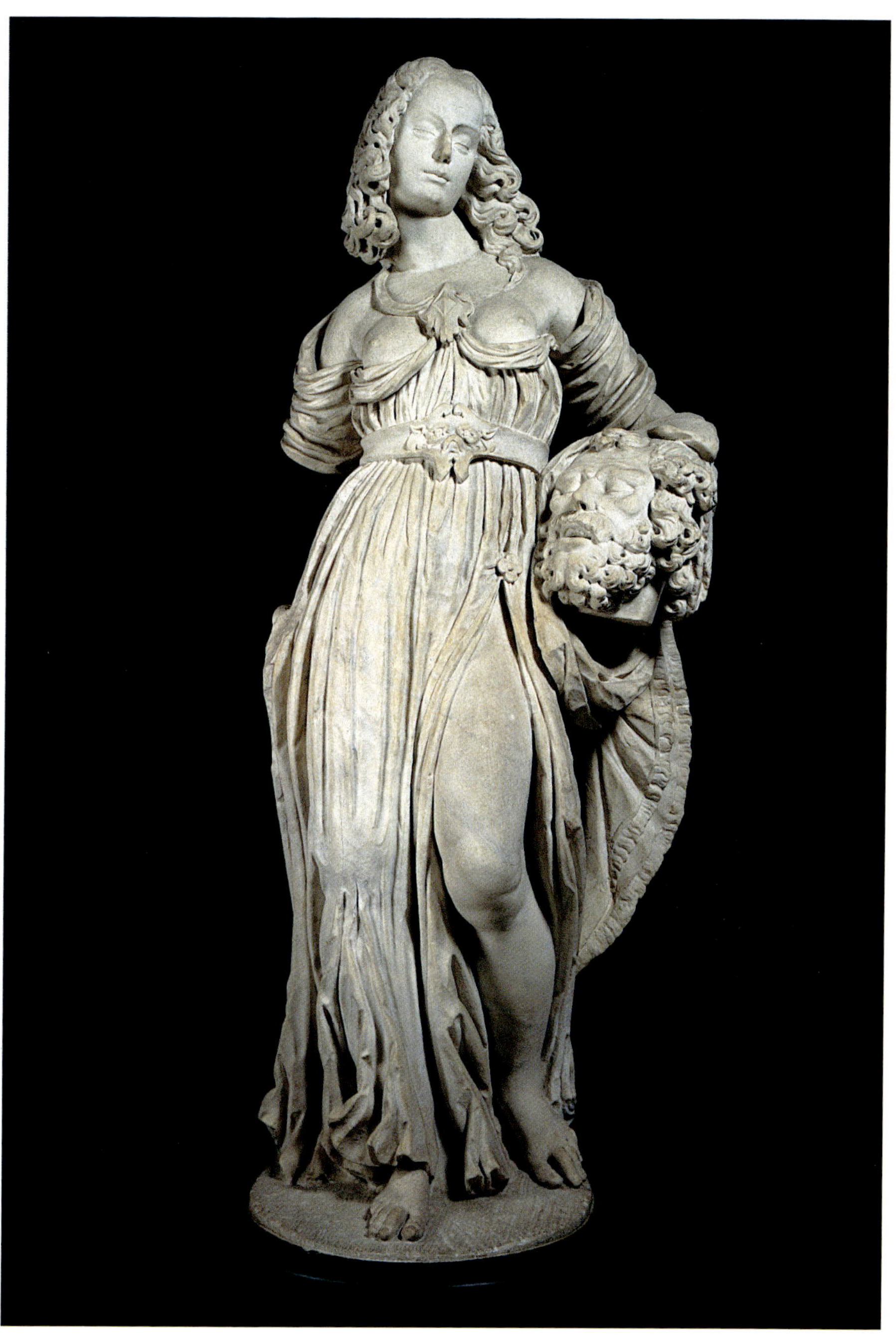

Wenceslaus Hollar

Arundel undertook an embassy to the Emperor Ferdinand II in 1636, and while passing through a Germany laid low as a result of the Thirty Years War ('the people are almost starved and daily die with grass in their mouth'), took into his service two individuals who were to play an important role with respect to his art collections. The painter Henry van der Borcht the Younger was to become curator of the Earl's pictures; and the talented engraver Wencelaus Hollar was to travel with the Earl and make sketches of places of interest that the party visited. The numerous drawings and etchings of views of German towns and cities attest to Hollar's industry in his new post. Even within days of engaging him, Arundel wrote to his agent William Petty in Venice: 'I have one Hollarse with me, whoe drawes and eches prints in strong water quickely, and with a pretty spiritte'.

Hollar accompanied Arundel back to England at the end of 1636 and lived in Arundel House, where he copied pieces in the Earl's collection, and also practiced on his own account, becoming drawing-master to the Prince of Wales (later Charles II). Hollar died in 1677, having produced thousands of prints, which included a series called *The Severall Habits of English Women.* After the Great Fire of London (1666) many buildings, in the words of John Aubrey, 'live now only in Mr. Hollar's etchings.'

Few prints can be attributed to Hollar's early years in London. He must, however, have been busy making numerous drawings, which he exploited when he went into exile in Antwerp with Alatheia (whose 'wayting-woman' he married in 1641). His sketchbooks served as his stock-in-trade for the rest of his career. Only one of the Arundel marbles seems to have been made into a print: the so-called 'Oxford Bust', erroneously identified as 'the empress Faustina, wife of Marcus Aurelius', and seen in mirror-image (Hollar frequently drew directly straight on to the copper plate), was published in Antwerp in 1645 (Vickers 1979b; Godfrey 1996; Harding 1996).

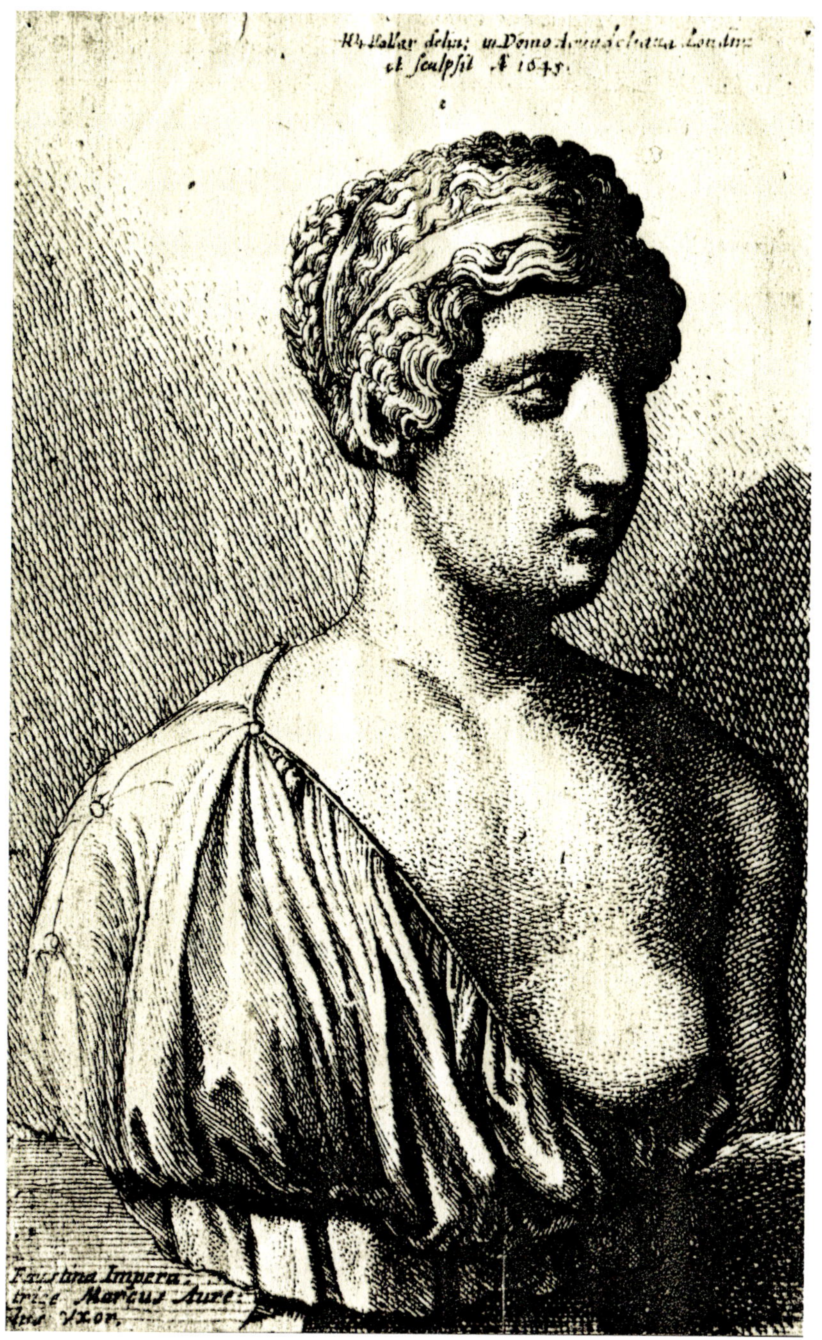

et sculpsit A 1645.
Faustina Impera:
trice Marcus Aure:
Vxor.

Death in Padua

Arundel spent his last years at Padua in northern Italy. John Evelyn saw him there in 1646, five months before his death. 'It was Easter Monday', he writes, 'that I was invited to Breakfast at the Earle of *Arundels*: I took leave of him in his bed, where I left that great & excellent Man in teares upon some private discourse of crosses that had befaln his Illustrious family: particularly the undutifulnesse of his *Grandson Philips* turning *Dominican* Friar (since *Cardinal of Norfolke*), the unkindnesse of his Countesse, now in Holland; The miseries of his Countrie, now embroil'd in a Civil War &c: after which he caused his Gentleman to give me Directions, all written with his owne hand, what curiosities I should enquire after in my Journey, & so injoyning me to write sometimes to him, I departed' (De Beer 1952, 2:79).

Whatever lay behind the estrangement between Arundel and his Countess, Alathea played the part of the sorrowing widow with honour and dignity, although she was never able to erect a suitable tomb in his memory. A simple plaque in the cloisters of the Santo in Padua is his only memorial (It begins 'Here lie the innards of Thomas Howard…').

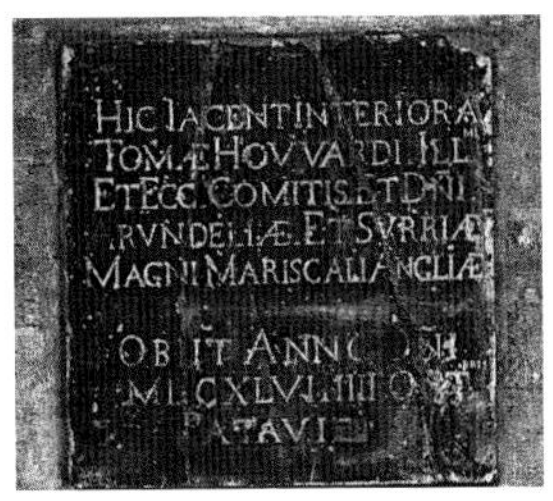

Above: Arundel's tombstone in the Santo, Padua.
Right: W.Hollar, *Apothesis of the Earl of Arundel*, *c*.1646.

We have a vivid impression of what an Arundel tomb monument might have looked like had the times been happier. Cornelius Schut conceived an apotheosis of Arundel in the Baroque manner (the original is in the Ashmolean), and it was engraved by Hollar. The Earl is seated on a sarcophagus, apparently set on the spina of a Roman circus: the race of life has been run. Time, Faith and Death pull the Earl in their several directions, while beneath him are Faith, Hope and Charity and personifications of Painting and Sculpture, with Athena coming actively to their aid. Classical statuary occupies the niches of the Circus, and Roman portrait heads lie on the ground. The inscription pays tribute to Alathea's piety and to her husband's learning and taste (Jaffé 1996, 31–2).

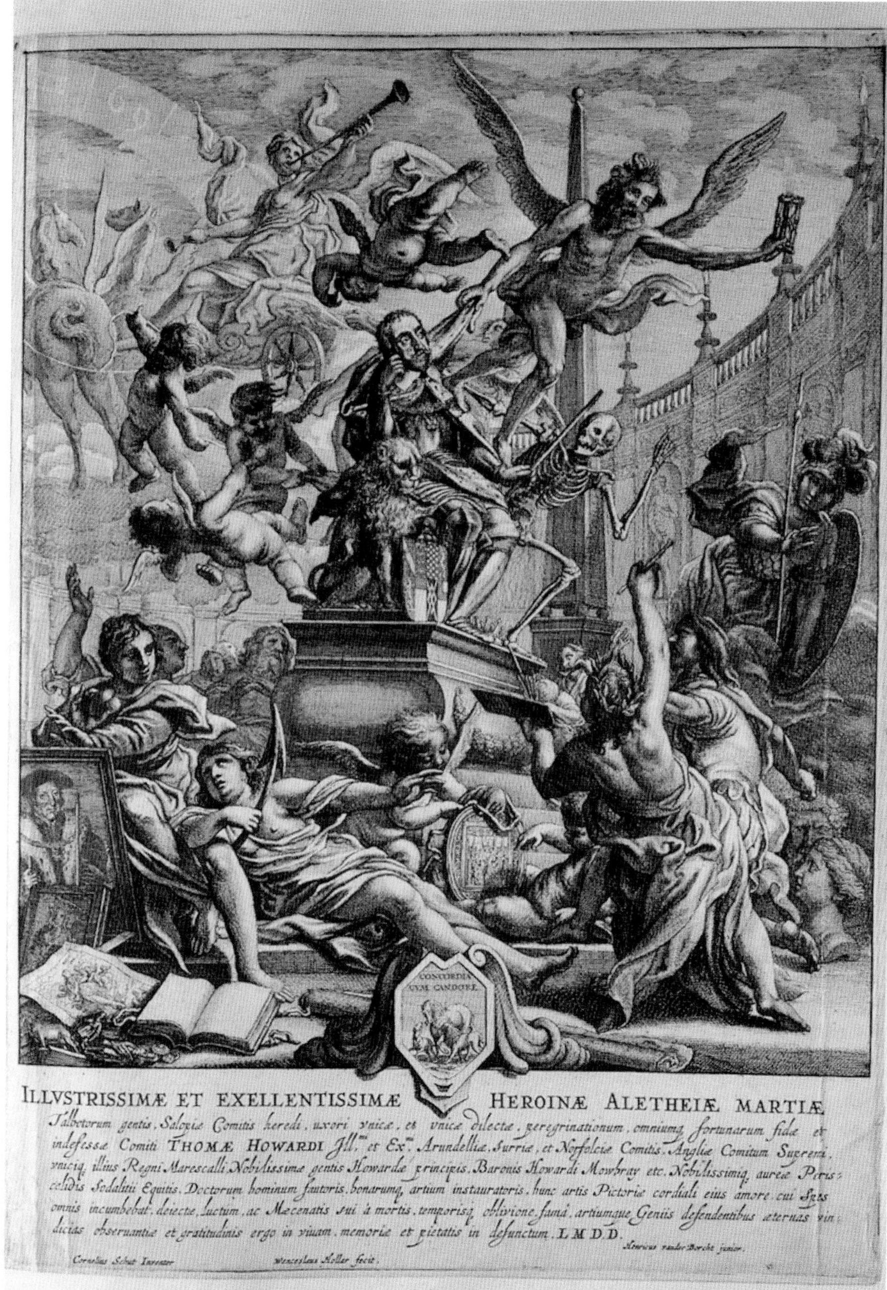
CONCORDIA
CVM CANDORE
ILLVSTRISSIMÆ ET EXELLENTISSIMÆ HEROINÆ ALETHEIÆ MARTIÆ
Talbotorum gentis, Salopiæ Comitis heredi, uxori vnicæ, et vnicæ dilectæ, peregrinationum, omniumq fortunarum fidæ et
indefessæ Comiti THOMÆ HOWARDI Jll.mi et Ex.mi Arundelliæ, Surriæ, et Norfolciæ Comitis, Angliæ Comitum Supremi,
vnicíq illius Regni Marescalli Nobilissimæ gentis Howardæ principis, Baronis Howardi Mowbray etc. Nobilissimiq aureæ Peris:
celidis Sodalitii Equitis, Doctorum hominum fautoris, bonarumq artium instauratoris, hunc artis Pictoriæ cordiali eius amore cui Spes
omnis incumbebat, deiectæ, luctum, ac Mæcenatis sui à mortis, temporisq oblivione, famâ, artiumque Geniis defendentibus æternas vin:
dicias obseruantiæ et gratitudinis ergo in viuam, memoriæ et pietatis in defunctum. L M D D.
Henricus vander Borcht junior.
Cornelius Schut Inventor
Wenceslaus Hollar fecit.

Selden and Arundel

When the inscriptions that Petty had acquired arrived in London in 1627, they generated great interest among Arundel's circle. Sir Robert Cotton, the famous librarian, encouraged the learned John Selden to set to work immediately on their decipherment. He readily did so, with the help of the Royal Librarian Patrick Young (Patricius Junius) and Richard James. They worked so diligently that Selden's *Marmora Arundeliana*, containing twenty-nine Greek inscriptions and ten Latin, appeared before the end of 1628 and spread the fame of the collection throughout learned Europe.

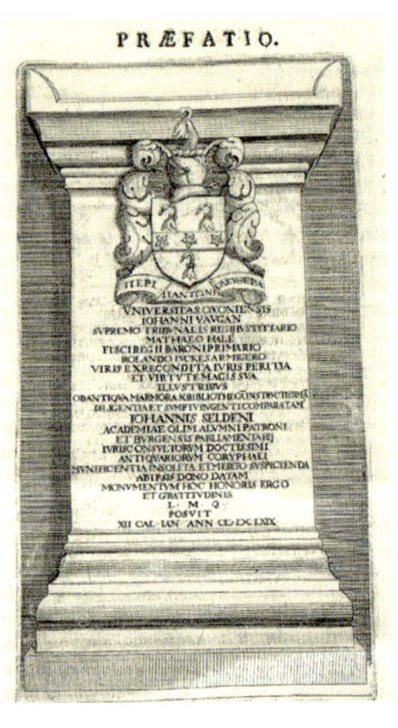

Selden (1584–1654) was, however, a collector in his own right, and was to bequeath to the University of Oxford his library and inscriptions. Around the time that the Arundel inscriptions arrived in Oxford in 1667 a slab was shaved off one of them (Chandler 2.30) to carry a Latin inscription to honour Selden's executors (cf. p. 38).

Selden's gift included two interesting reliefs. One (Michaelis 136; H.: 49 cm, W.: 1.58 m) shows horsemen wearing protective clothing taking part in a sport which was popular in Roman Thessaly and Asia Minor, namely Taurokathapsis, or bull wrestling. The bulls were chased on horseback, and the rider would seize one by the horns and wrestle it to the ground. Another relief from Smyrna (where this relief was found, in the sea) shows a competitor with a prostrate bull raising his hand in triumph. The inscription reads 'The second day of the Taurokathapsis festival'. The other relief (Michaelis 137; H.: 99 cm, W.: 59 cm) has graphic scenes of chain gangs of slaves and animals destined for circus games.

Engravings of the Selden inscription, the *Taurokathapsis* and *Slaves* from H. Prideaux, *Marmora Oxoniensia* (1676), pp. x, 266–7, and 104.

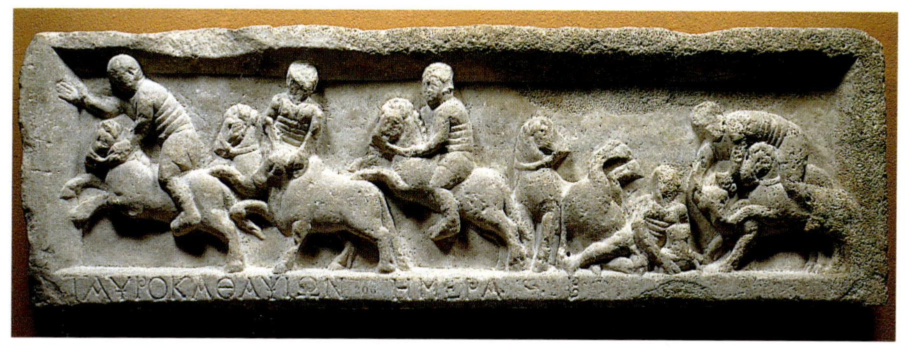

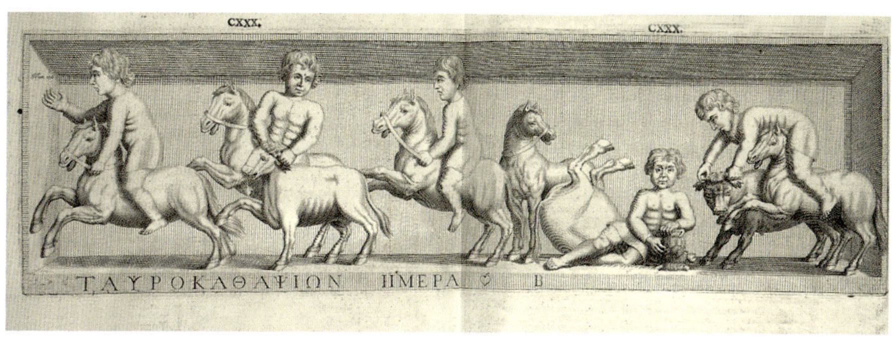
CXXX.
CXXX.
ΤΑΥΡΟΚΑΘΑΨΙΩΝ ΗΜΕΡΑ Β

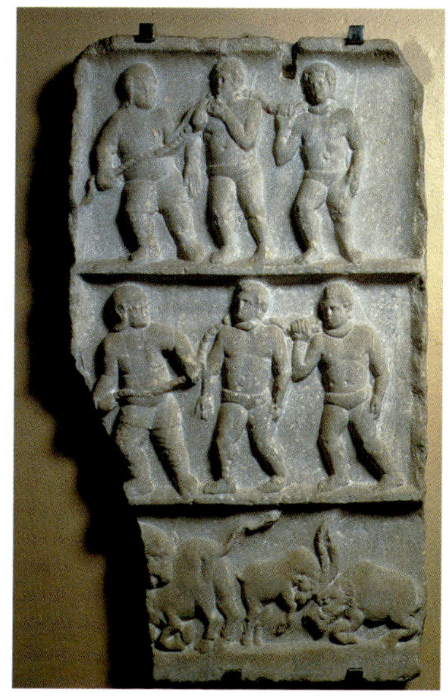

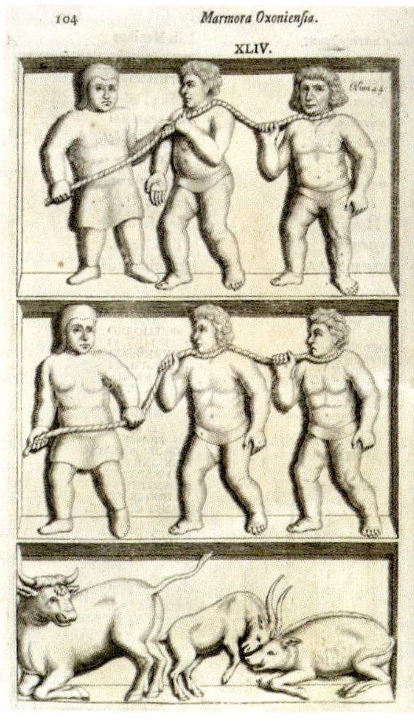
104 Marmora Oxoniensia.
XLIV.

Howard gift

After the Civil War the diarist Evelyn rather crustily complained that Henry Howard, Arundel's grandson, filled the house with 'painters, panders and misses'. (The house was actually used by the newly founded Royal Society.) Of the two hundred and fifty inscriptions collected by Arundel one hundred and fourteen had already gone when Evelyn intervened to save the rest. 'These precious monuments' he writes in his *Diary* for September 19, 1667, 'when I saw miserably neglected & scattred up & downe about the Gardens and other places of Arundell-house, & how exceedingly the corrosive aire of *London* Impaired them, I procured him to bestow on the *Universite of Oxford*; this he was pleased to grant me, & now gave me the key of the Gallery, with leave to mark all those stones, Urnes, Altars &c; & whatever I found had inscriptions on them that were not Status; This I did, & getting them removed and piled together, with those which were incrusted in the Garden walles, I sent immediately letters to the *Vice-Chancellor* what I had procured, & that if they esteemed it a service to the *University* (of which I had been a member) they should take orders for their transportation'.

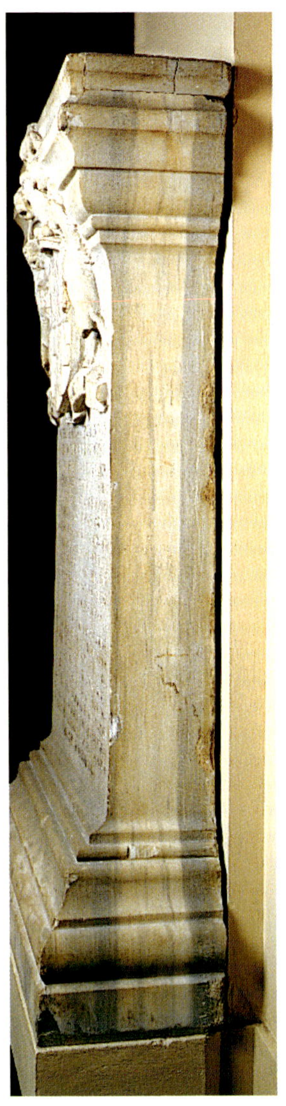

The inscriptions duly arrived and a grateful university commemorated the gift with a grandiloquent inscription listing Henry Howard's titles and those of his illustrious ancestor, who is said to have liberated the Arundel marbles from 'Ottoman barbarism'. The university authorities solved the problem of finding marble for the monument by the simple expedient of cutting a slice off the back of a large Roman-period Greek inscription from Asia Minor (in fact, Chandler 2.30). A glance at the edge shows that it is made from Proconnesian marble with its characteristic dark streaks.

Engraving of the Howard inscription from H. Prideaux, *Marmora Oxoniensia* (1676), p. ix.

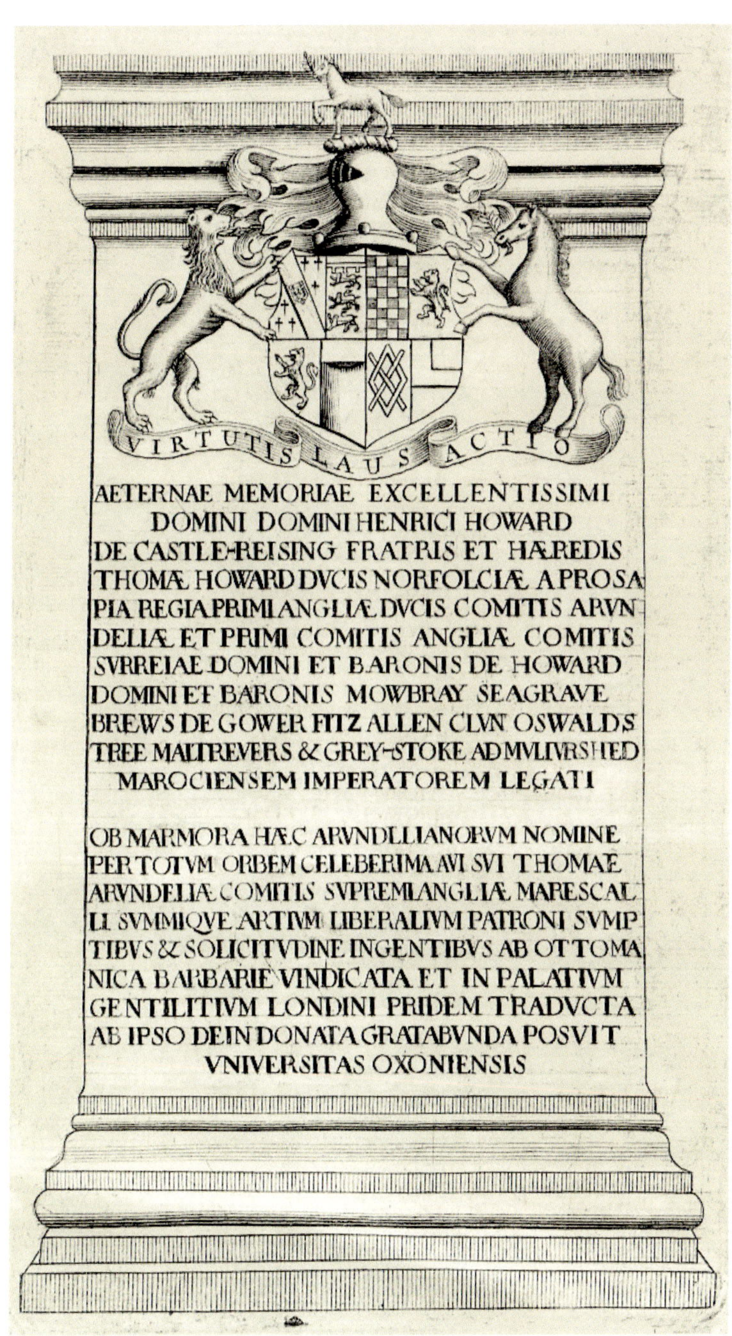
VIRTUTIS LAUS ACTIO
AETERNAE MEMORIAE EXCELLENTISSIMI
DOMINI DOMINI HENRICI HOWARD
DE CASTLE-REISING FRATRIS ET HÆREDIS
THOMÆ HOWARD DVCIS NORFOLCIÆ A PROSA
PIA REGIA PRIMI ANGLIÆ DVCIS COMITIS ARVN
DELIÆ ET PRIMI COMITIS ANGLIÆ COMITIS
SVRREIAE DOMINI ET BARONIS DE HOWARD
DOMINI ET BARONIS MOWBRAY SEAGRAVE
BREWS DE GOWER FITZ ALLEN CLVN OSWALDS
TREE MALTREVERS & GREY-STOKE AD MVLIVRSHED
MAROCIENSEM IMPERATOREM LEGATI
OB MARMORA HÆC ARVNDLLIANORVM NOMINE
PER TOTVM ORBEM CELEBERIMA AVI SVI THOMAE
ARVNDELIÆ COMITIS SVPREMI ANGLIÆ MARESCAL
LI SVMMIQVE ARTIVM LIBERALIVM PATRONI SVMP
TIBVS & SOLICITVDINE INGENTIBVS AB OTTOMA
NICA BARBARIE VINDICATA ET IN PALATIVM
GENTILITIVM LONDINI PRIDEM TRADVCTA
AB IPSO DEIN DONATA GRATABVNDA POSVIT
VNIVERSITAS OXONIENSIS

Arundel Inscriptions in Oxford

Between 1660 and 1715 there was a 'Garden of Antiquities' in the space around the Sheldonian Theatre. At first it housed the inscriptions that John Selden had bequeathed to the University, but in 1668–9 it was greatly enlarged to accommodate Henry Howard's gift. It is likely that Christopher Wren, Professor of Astronomy in the University, and the architect of the Sheldonian Theatre (inaugurated 1669) was behind the new design. The flanking walls of the Sheldonian were adorned with a series of bays, which served as showcases for the inscriptions that were placed there. It is possible that the arrangement of the inscriptions themselves was put in the hands of Henry Aldrich (later to be Dean of Christ Church), for a proof-engraving was found amongst his papers showing one panel and its contents as they appeared in about 1675. More than a hundred inscriptions were thus immured.

John Evelyn had been instrumental in getting the Arundel inscriptions to Oxford, and took an interest in their welfare once they had been installed. He observed that 'people, approaching them too neare, some Idle people began to Scratch and injure some of them, I advis'd that an hedge of holly, should be planted at the foote of the wall, to be kept breast-high only, to protect them, which the *V. Chancellor* promised to see don next season' (*Diary*, July 13, 1669). Excavations in 1992 revealed the existence of small trenches for the holly bushes (Sturdy and Moorcraft 1999).

The task of publishing the inscriptions was entrusted to Humphrey Prideaux of Christ Church. His work appeared in 1676 as *Marmora Oxoniensia*. A copy preserved in the Ashmolean was presented by the Vice-Chancellor Randolph Bathurst to Elias Ashmole, the founder in 1683 of the Museum in which they are now housed.

Above: Howard inscriptions at the Sheldonian, *c.*1675.
Below: Title page of Prideaux's *Marmora Oxoniensia*, 1676

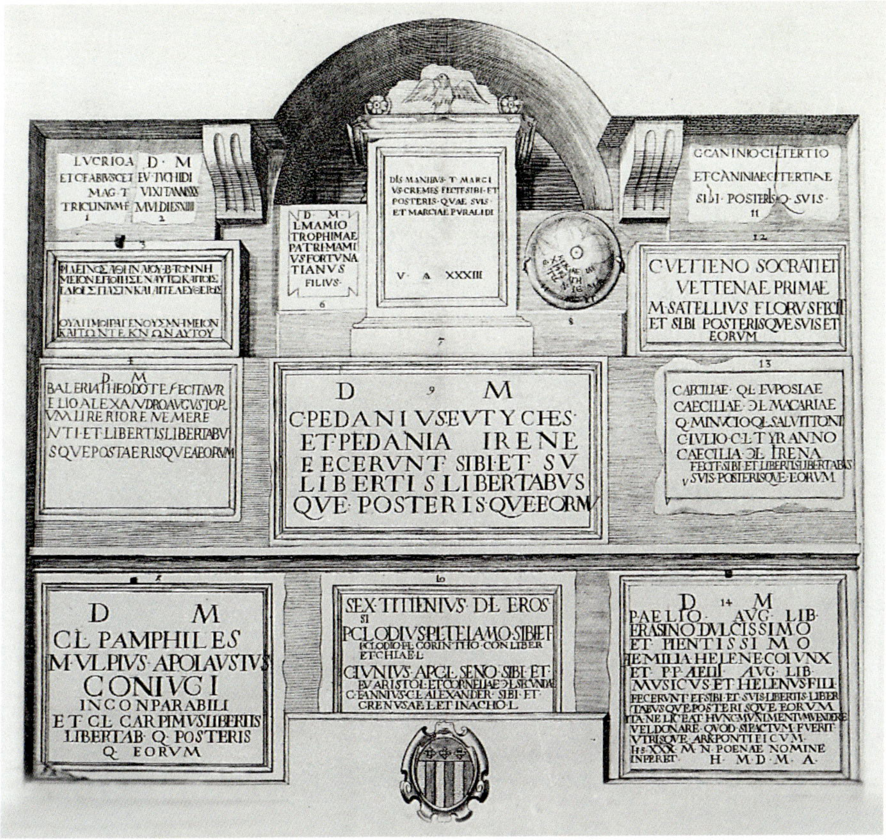

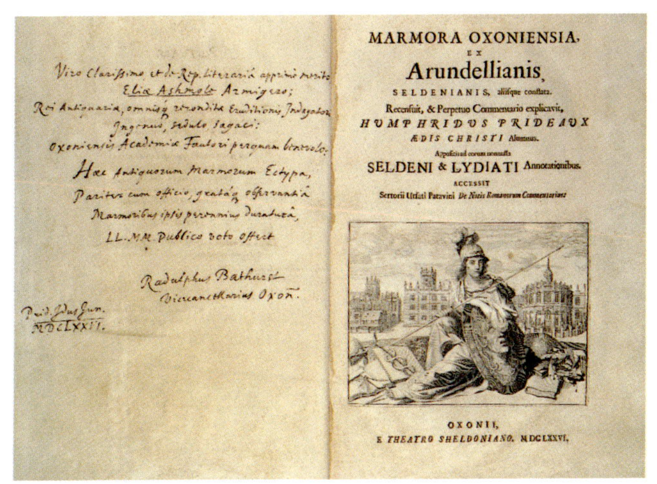

Viro Clarissimo et de Rep. literariâ apprime merito
Eliæ Ashmole Armigero;
Rei Antiquariæ, omnisq; reconditæ Eruditionis Indagatori
Ingenuo, sedulo, sagaci:
Oxoniensis Academiæ Fautori pergnam benevolo.
Hæc Antiquorum Marmorum Ectypa,
Pariter cum officio, gratâq; observantiâ
Marmoribus ipsis perennius duraturâ,
LL.MM. Publico voto offert
Radulphus Bathurst
Vicecancellarius Oxon.

MDCLXXVI.

MARMORA OXONIENSIA,
EX
Arundellianis,
SELDENIANIS, aliisque conflata.
Recensuit, & Perpetuo Commentario explicavit,
HUMPHRIDUS PRIDEAUX
ÆDIS CHRISTI Alumnus.
Appositis ad eorum nonnulla
SELDENI & LYDIATI Annotationibus.
ACCESSIT
Sertorii Ursati Patavini De Notis Romanorum Commentarius

OXONII,
E THEATRO SHELDONIANO. MDCLXXVI.

Latin Tombstone

c. AD 100
H.: 61 cm
Howard gift 1667 Chandler 3.34

Valerius Paternus had served as a *speculator* in the Roman army in Britain some time around the end of the first, or the beginning of the second, century AD. *Speculatores* were part of the governor's staff, ten being taken from each legion in the province. They served as a kind of military police force and their duties included the custody and execution of prisoners, and the delivery of messages to Rome. After his retirement Valerius returned to Rome where he died and where this inscription was originally erected. It figured among the many Greek and Latin inscriptions from the Arundel collection given to the University of Oxford in 1667.

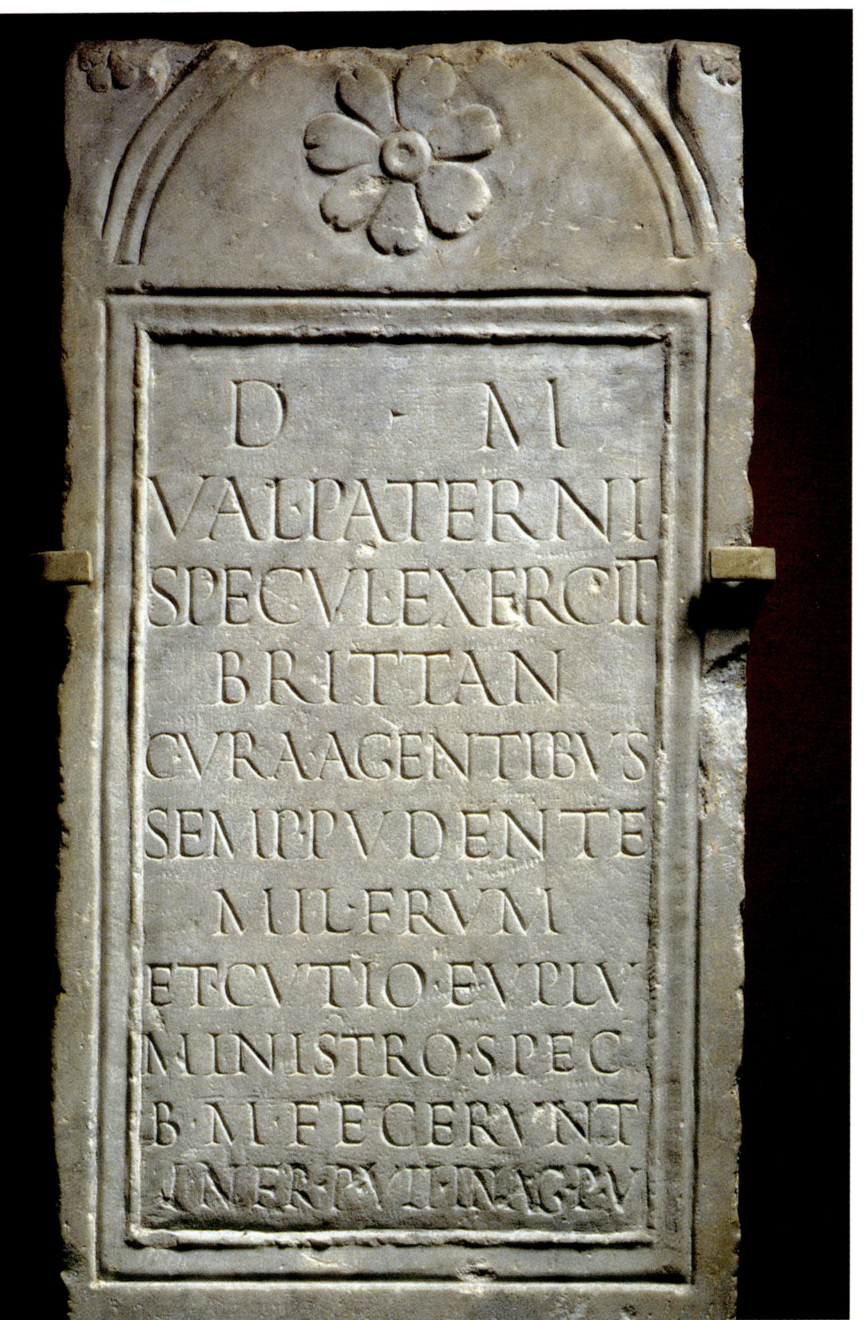
D · M
VAL·PATERNI
SPECVL·EXERCIT
BRITTAN
CVRA AGENTIBVS
SEM·P·PVDENTE
MIL·FRVM
ET CVTIO·EVPLV
MINISTRO·SPEC
B·M·FECERVNT

Easton Neston

The statues (as opposed to the inscriptions) remained in the grounds of Arundel House until 1691, when they were bought by Sir William Fermor (later Lord Lempster) for £300 to decorate the grounds of his new house at Easton Neston in Northamptonshire. His son Thomas was made Earl of Pomfret in 1721.

Drawings by Peter Tillemans in the British Library show many of the Arundel marbles at Easton Neston (Bailey 1996), and a description by George Vertue made in 1734 gives a good idea of how the sculptures were used to adorn the gardens. A special feature was 'Germanicus's tomb' centred on a sarcophagus which in Arundel House had once supported a bust said to be that of Germanicus, and which owed its name to this flimsy tale:

> ... upon the tomb is set a round pedestal, and on that a marble statue of Jupiter less than the life; one each side of this pedestal are fine bustos of two women [one of them the 'Oxford Bust'; see p. 59], and on each side of this arch or alcove are doric pilasters, which support a pediment, in which there is in basso relievo the figure of a man as big as the life, with his arms extended as if he was crucified, but no lower than about his paps is seen, the cornice cutting him off as it were; and this extension of his arms is called a grecian measure, and over his right arm is a grecian foot [the 'Metrological Relief'; see p. 63]; on the top of the pediment stands the god Terminus, and likewise on each side of this alcove are two smaller niches; in that on the left hand, as you look to the tomb, is the trunk of a body, the fore part towards you; and in that on the right hand, a trunk of a body, the back towards you, the proportion and muscles very fine, and both well executed; so as to be worthy a sculptor's study [see p. 61]
> (Vertue 1758, 55–6; cf. Vickers 1988–89).

Right: Peter Tillemans, *Germanicus's Tomb at Easton Neston*, 1719, British Library

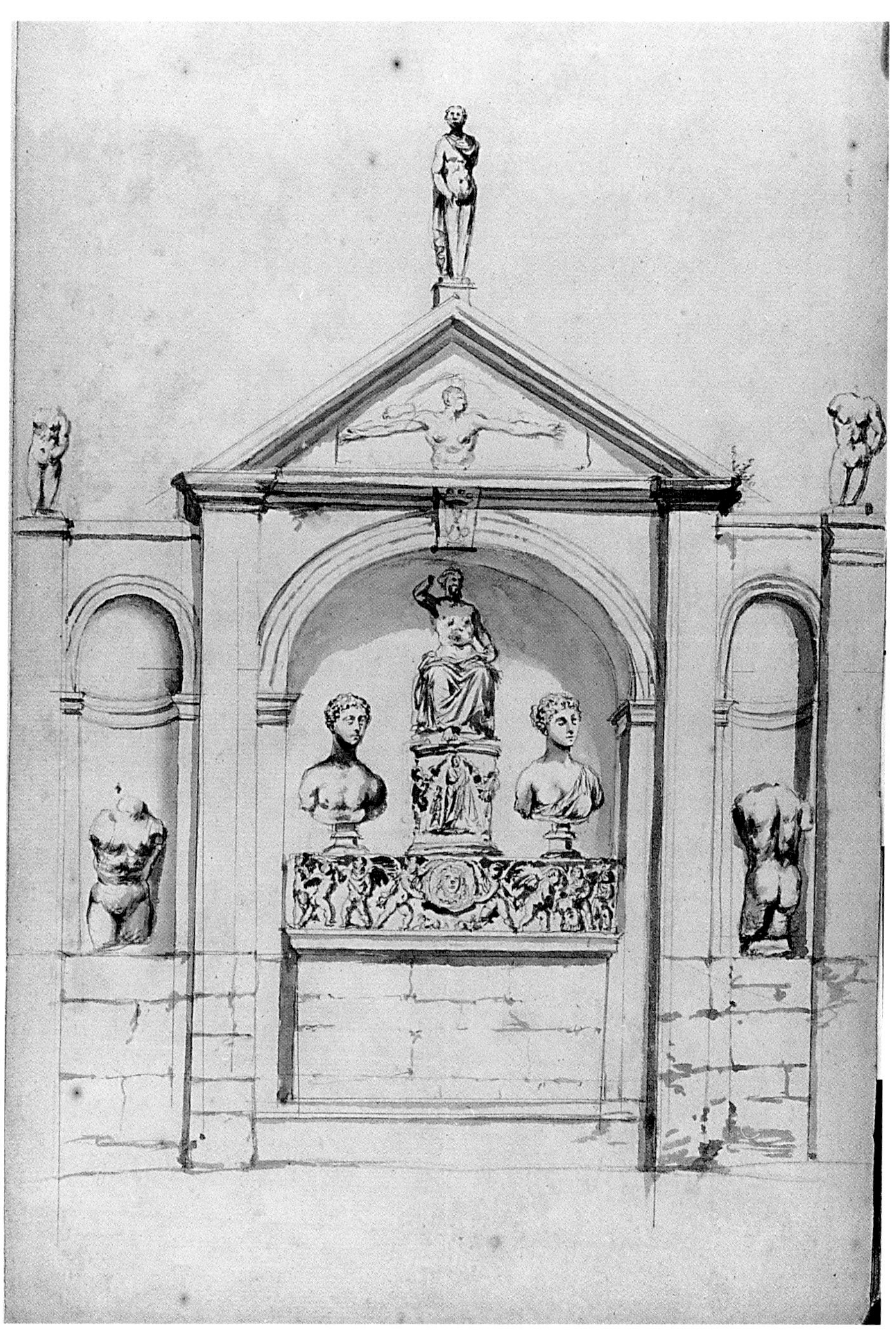

Giovanni Battista Guelfi

Some time after 1720, Thomas Fermor, later first Earl of Pomfret, who had visited Rome, engaged the Italian sculptor Giovanni Battista Guelfi (born *c.*1690) to restore the Arundel marbles. He was a native of Bergamo and had learned his craft in Rome under Camillo Rusconi (Giometti 1999). The results of his restoration were disastrous since Guelfi 'misconceived the character and attitude of almost every statue he attempted to make perfect; and ruined a greater number of those he was permitted to touch' (Dallaway 1800, 237). This is the universal view of Guelfi's work, for although he was 'much opinionated, and as an Italian thought no body could be equal to himself in skill in this Country. Yet all his works seem to the judicious very often defective, wanting spirit and grace' (Vertue 1934, 74). The task 'could not easily have been entrusted to more unfortunate hands. Great as has been the blundering perpetrated in all quarters in the shape of so-called "restorations", yet hardly ever have any antiques been so shamefully tampered with as in the tasteless additions made by this shallow botcher' (Michaelis 1882, 39). The Venus illustrated here (Pomfret gift, Michaelis 10, H.: 1.04m) is a typical example of the work of Guelfi, who was otherwise employed by Lord Burlington who, it was said parted with Guelfi 'very willingly' when the latter returned to Italy in 1734. Several of his funerary monuments still survive (Webb 1995).

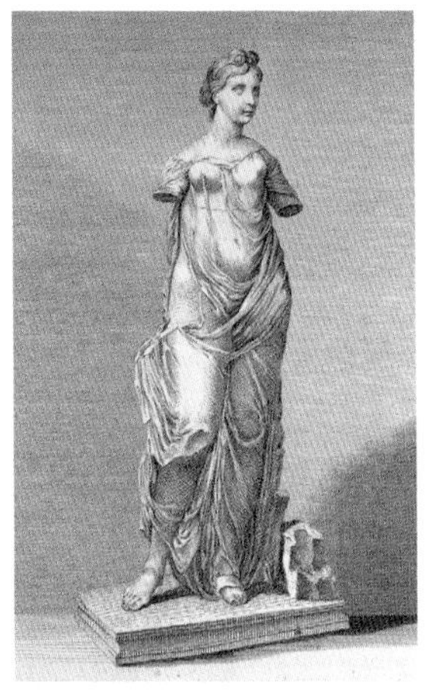

Above: Engraving of Venus from R. Chandler, *Marmora Oxoniensia* (1763).
Right: *Venus* restored by G.B. Guelfi.

Most of Guelfi's restorations can be seen in J. Miller's illustrations in Richard Chandler's *Marmora Oxoniensia* of 1763, but they were understandably removed in the nineteenth century. The statue of Venus shown here was temporarily restored for photography for this booklet. The upper part was added by Guelfi.

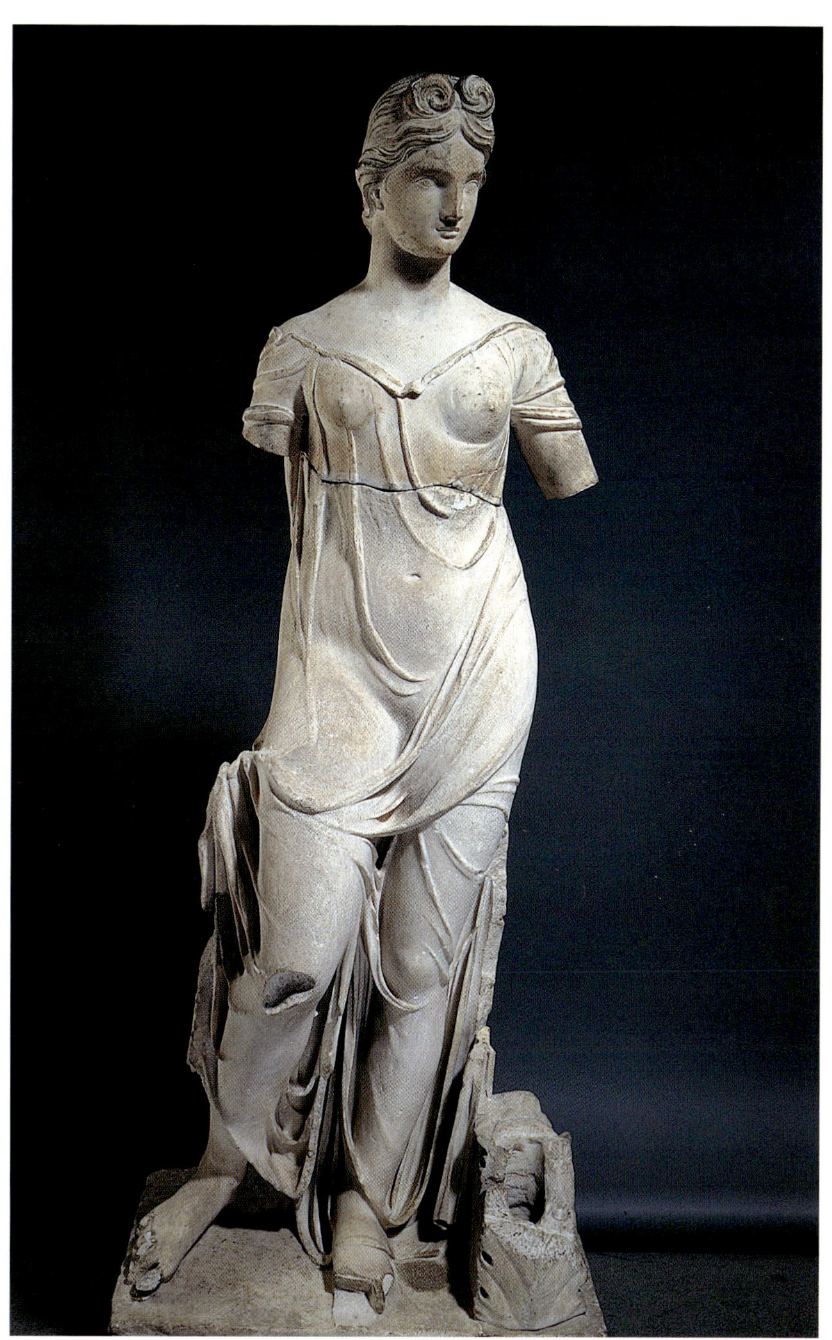

Sphinxes

First–third century AD
H.: 54 cm; L.: 1.13 m
Pomfret gift 1755 Michaelis 56

Eighteenth century
H.: 59 cm; L.: 1.10 m
Pomfret gift 1755 Michaelis 57; Penny 1992, No. 518

Sphinxes came into fashion in the Roman world after Augustus defeated the forces of Antony and Cleopatra at the battle of Actium in 30 B.C. Augustus became the de *facto* pharaoh of Egypt, and to employ the image of one of the most characteristic mythical creatures of Egypt was a nice way to display loyalty to the regime. They occur throughout the Roman empire until the 3rd century AD. Sphinxes were set up in pairs at either side of entrances to guard the passageway, and also figured as guardians of graves.

There were two sphinxes among the Pomfret marbles. One is of Roman origin, while the other was made in more recent times. Both are shown *couchant* wearing an Egyptian headcloth surmounted by a miniature Double Crown; over their chests lie broad collars. It is uncertain whether the 'new' (slightly larger) piece was made for Arundel House or for Easton Neston. It is certainly the case, however, that there are two very similar Portland stone sphinxes by Guelfi at Chiswick House, after which a lead sphinx there was made by John Cleere (Penny 1992, No. 518)

Above: Roman sphinx.
Below: 18th-century sphinx

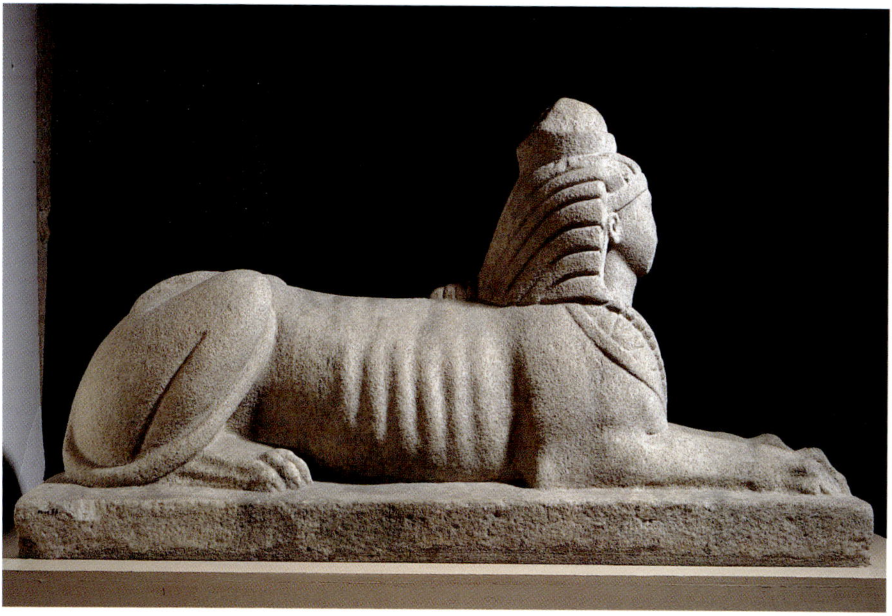

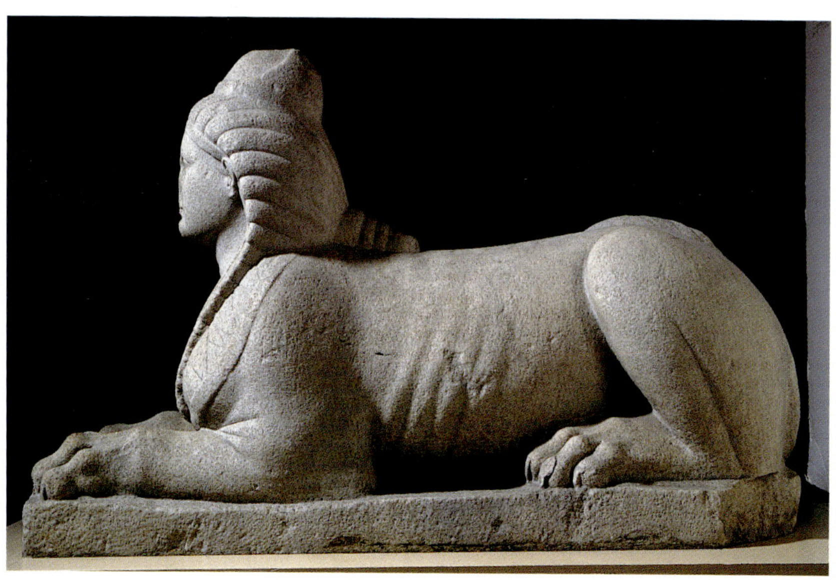

The Pomfret Gift to Oxford

William Fermor, first Earl of Pomfret died in 1753, and was succeeded by his son George. His debts were so great that he was obliged to sell all his movable assets, and the Arundel sculpture at Easton Neston was bought by his mother, the Dowager Countess Henrietta Louisa. She, however, was a convert to Gothic revivalism, and presented the collection of classical statues to the University of Oxford in 1755. Already in 1751, she and her husband chose to place their portrait by Thomas Bardwell in a Gothic frame, and in 1757, she built a large town house (Pomfret House) in Arlington Street in a strikingly Gothic style. With its traceried walls and fan-vaulted ceilings, it recalled the middle ages rather than the classical past (Houfe 1977). When she died in 1761, she was buried in the University Church at Oxford, appropriately commemorated with a Gothic monument (Colvin 1994). Horace Walpole (himself a leader of the Gothic revival movement) ridiculed the countess's 'paltry air of significant learning and absurdity', adding that she was so totally lacking in humour that 'she repined when she should laugh and reasoned when she should be diverted'. Nevertheless, it is thanks to her that a major part of the Arundel collection was saved from dispersal and eventually reunited with the Arundel inscriptions that were already in Oxford; verses composed for the occasion included the lines:

> The sculptur'd column, and the breathing bust,
> Stand here, deliver'd from oblivion's dust. (Mytton 1758, 7)

At the same time there probably came a pair of marble portraits of the Earl and Countess of Pomfret, 'the best surviving works by Guelfi in this country' (Penny 1992, Nos 516, 517).

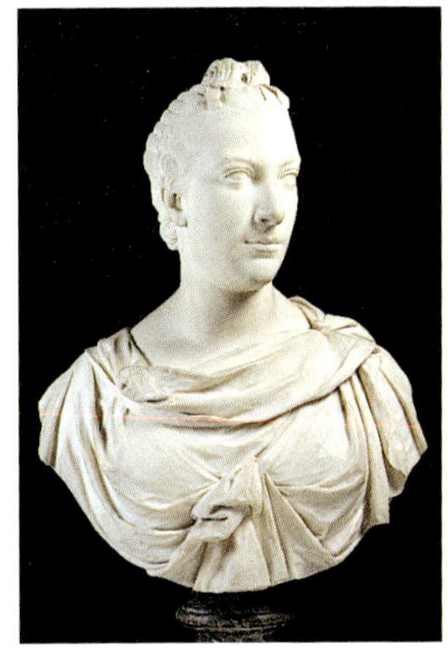

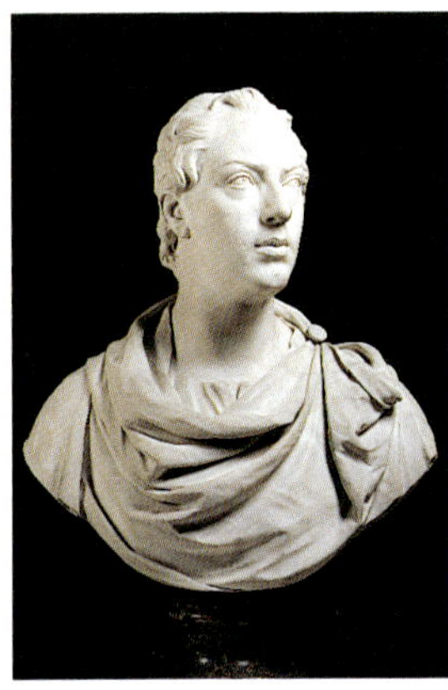

Above: Giovanni Battista Guelfi, *Earl and Countess of Pomfret.* Right: Thomas Bardwell, *Earl and Countess of Pomfret* (1751)

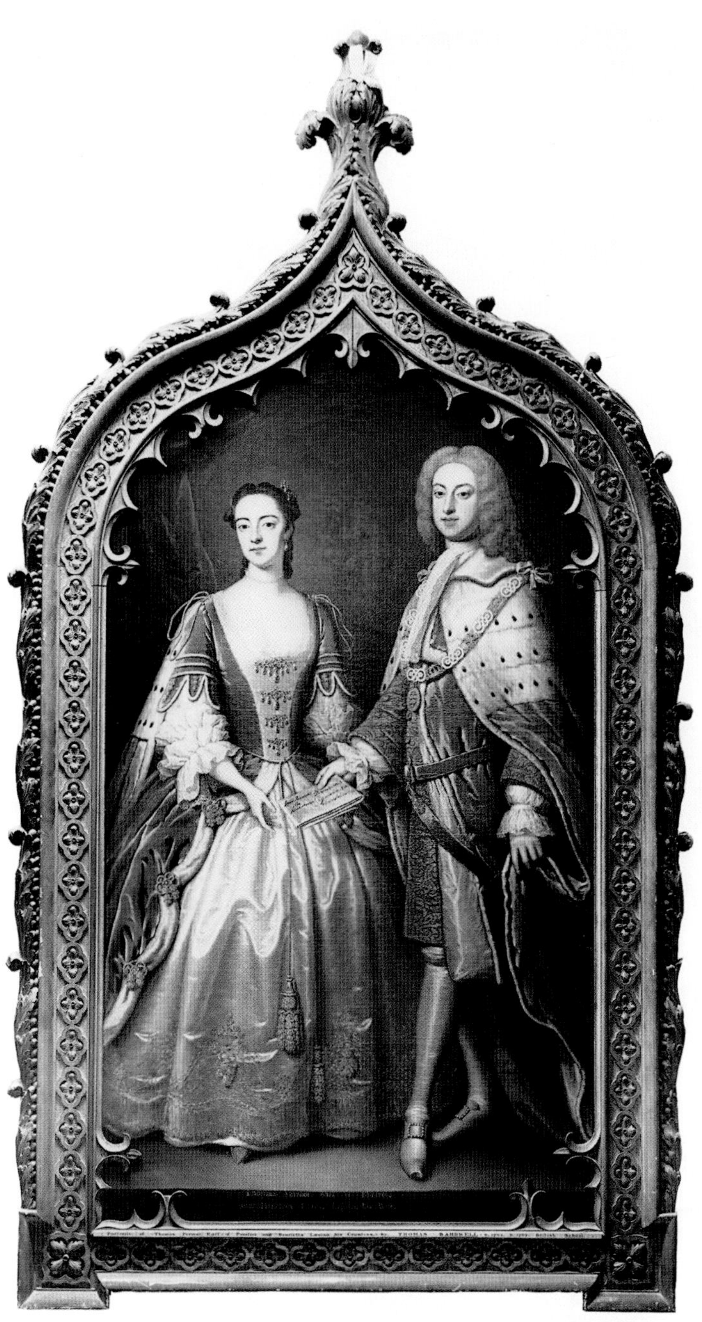

The Arrival of the Pomfret Marbles in Oxford

Every year, the University of Oxford publishes a ceremonial calendar illustrating some new building or important gift. The University Almanack for 1757 shows a fanciful view of the Pomfret Marbles arriving in Oxford in 1755. Many pieces can be recognised: the 'Cicero', the Metrological relief, the Sphinx. The caption reads:

> The Design of the Plate is to exhibit the Connexion of the Studies of Antiquity, Sculpture, and Architecture, with what is usually called academical Learning. To this End the University, attended by her three Faculties, is introduced from her Gothic retirement by Minerva to the Knowledge of these Arts; represented by three Groupes of allegorical Figures. In one of which, Time is endeavouring to destroy an old Marble, containing the Smyrnaean Decree, and League with the Magnesians, preserved at OXFORD in the ARUNDEL Collection; but is prevented by the Genius of antique Learning, who leads up History to consult the Inscription. In another, Sculpture is explaining to the Genius of classical Learning a beautiful Bas-Relief of the Destruction of Troy, in the Collection lately presented to the University by the Countess of Pomfret. In the third, Architecture is consulting with Geometry on the Plan of a Building, destined for the Reception of these once more united Collections. On the Cornice of a ruined Amphitheatre, and in other parts of the Plate, are casually disposed the Cicero, the Marius, the Roman Foot and Fathom, the Graecian Epochae, the Delphic Column and Capital, the Bacchus, Hercules, and many other of the ARUNDEL and POMFRET Marbles (Petter 1974, 68–9).

It is interesting to note that the message, with its implicit rejection of Gothicism, is in direct contrast to the donor's tastes and interests. The University's implied promise to give the collection a dignified home was only to be fulfilled with the construction of the University Galleries (now the Ashmolean Museum) in the 1840s.

Oxford University Almanack (1757)

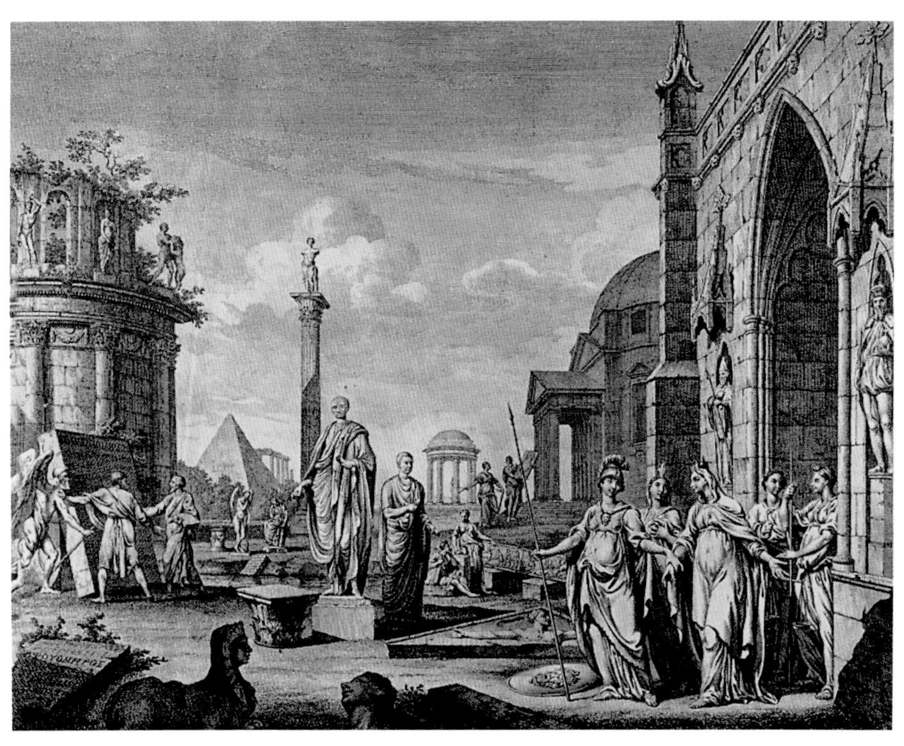

Winckelmann's Column

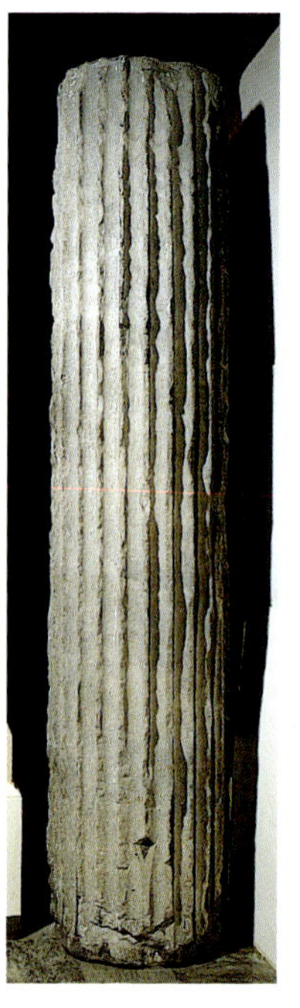

Third century BC–2nd century AD
H.: 2.27 m
Pomfret gift

Michaelis 130

In 1756, the German art-historian J.J. Winckelmann (right) wrote somewhat ironically of the way in which relics of classical antiquity were carried away from their original homes, so that 'there are even columns from the Temple of Apollo on Delos in English gardens' ('Die Denkmale des Alterthums werden von Zeit zu Zeit noch mehr vertilget, theils weggeführet; und in englischen Gärten stehen itzo Säulen von dem Tempel des Apollo zu Delos.' Uhlig 1982, 83). These words allude to, and exaggerate, the role played by English collectors of antiquities in Winckelmann's day. The specific allusion, however, is to a column that Lord Lempster had erected at Easton Neston, and which was recorded by William Stukeley, the antiquary, as follows:

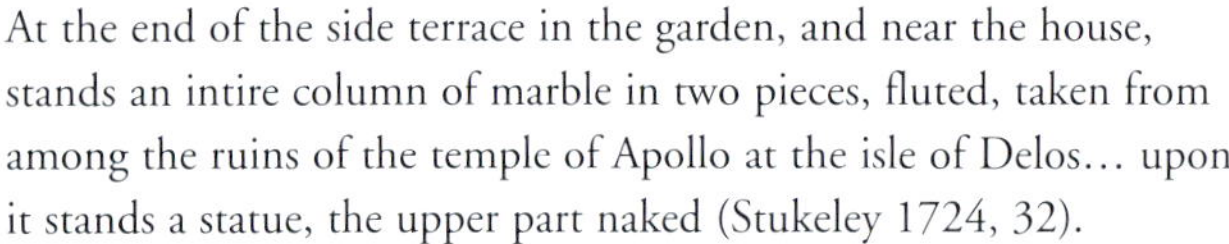

> At the end of the side terrace in the garden, and near the house, stands an intire column of marble in two pieces, fluted, taken from among the ruins of the temple of Apollo at the isle of Delos… upon it stands a statue, the upper part naked (Stukeley 1724, 32).

The Delian origin is purely speculative, for when the same column came to Oxford (it is prominent in the Almanac view), it was described as a 'column from Delphos' (Chandler 1763, 8). On balance Delos is more likely in that the site was more accessible to travellers, and Petty was probably active there in 1625 and 1626 (Michaelis 1882, 187–200; Lapierre 2004). The Delphian attribution need have no more basis in reality than the 'tomb of Germanicus', and Delphos was probably a mistake for Delos, as Michaelis already saw (Michaelis 1882, 572; Vickers, forthcoming).

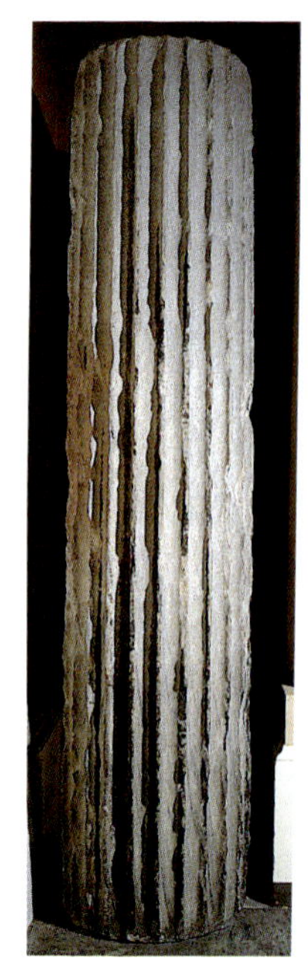

The statue of Apollo could not be located when Adolf Michaelis visited Oxford in 1881 (Michaelis 1882, 555). But the two column fragments did come here, as did the capital. The shafts can today be seen in the Museum's Randolph Sculpture Gallery, awkwardly tucked away in a corner; but these neglected stumps can now be seen for what they are: harbingers of the truly splendid acquisitions made by the unjustly maligned Lord Elgin two centuries later.

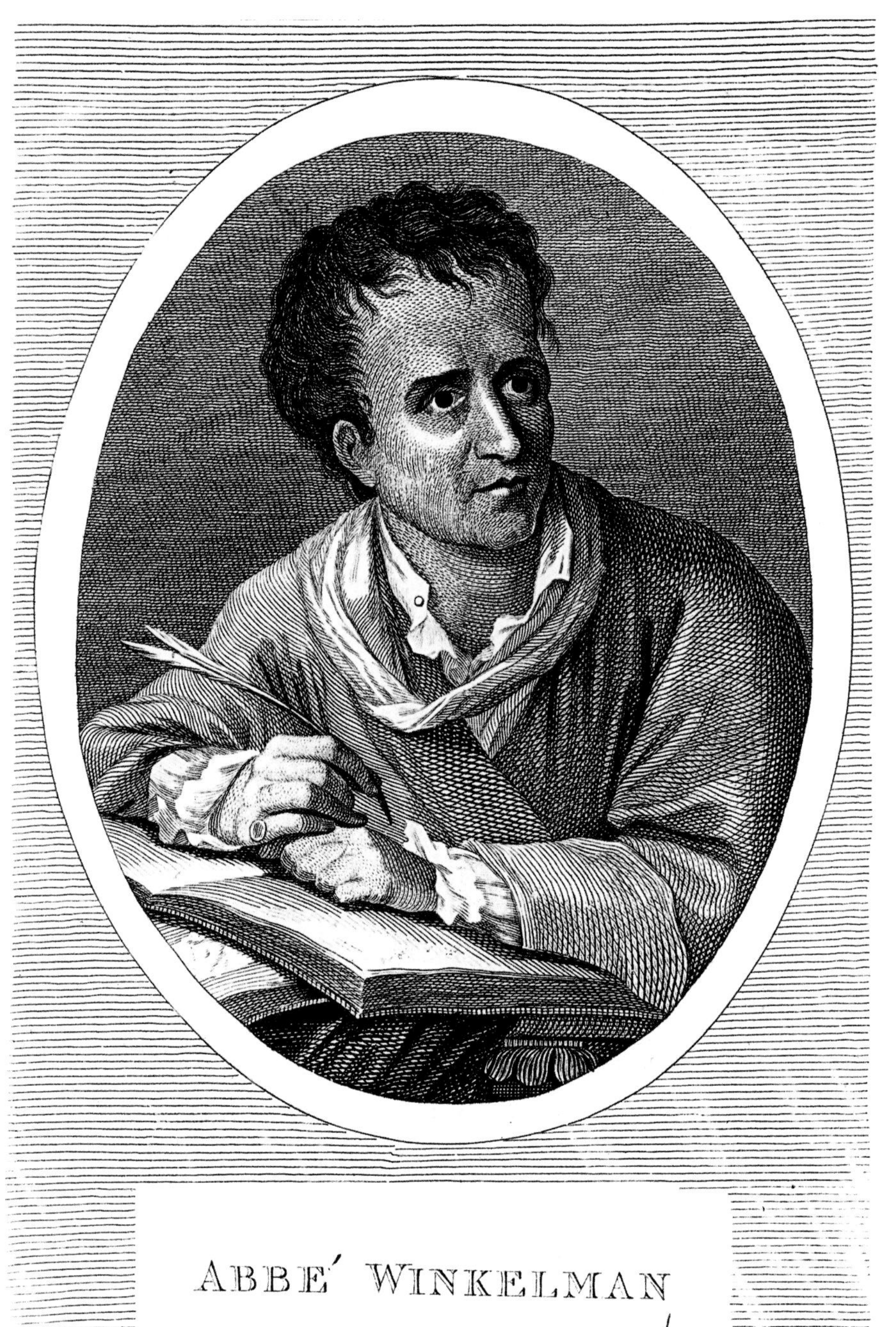

ABBE′ WINKELMAN

The Old Schools

After their arrival in Oxford, the Arundel/Pomfret Marbles had to wait for nearly a century before they were displayed in a purpose-built sculpture gallery. They were placed for the moment on an upper floor of the Old Schools (now the Bodleian Library). A watercolour sketch by William Westall (made for inclusion in Rudolph Ackermann's *A History of the University of Oxford* [1814]) shows the collection in their temporary home. The colossal Athena (Michaelis 19, see p. 79) dominated the room; her large scale is emphasized by the presence of the human figures at her feet. On the shelf to the right we can recognize Henry VIII (see p. 19) and Prince Rupert of the Rhine (see p. 28). The file of statues on the left includes an Eros (Michaelis 36), a seated Muse (Michaelis 32), and a Wounded Amazon (Michaelis 24; see p. 69); those on the right, a barbarian in a Phrygian cap (Michaelis 48), another Muse (Michaelis 31), and Guelfi's Venus (Michaelis 10, see p. 47). 'Cicero' (see p. 15) stands behind the wooden chair.

It was only in 1845 that the Pomfret gifts were moved to C.R. Cockerell's newly built University Galleries, the present Ashmolean Museum, where most of them are now exhibited in the Randolph Gallery.

Above: William Westall, *Old Schools*, watercolour sketch (1813)
Below: from R. Ackermann, *A History of the University of Oxford* (1814)

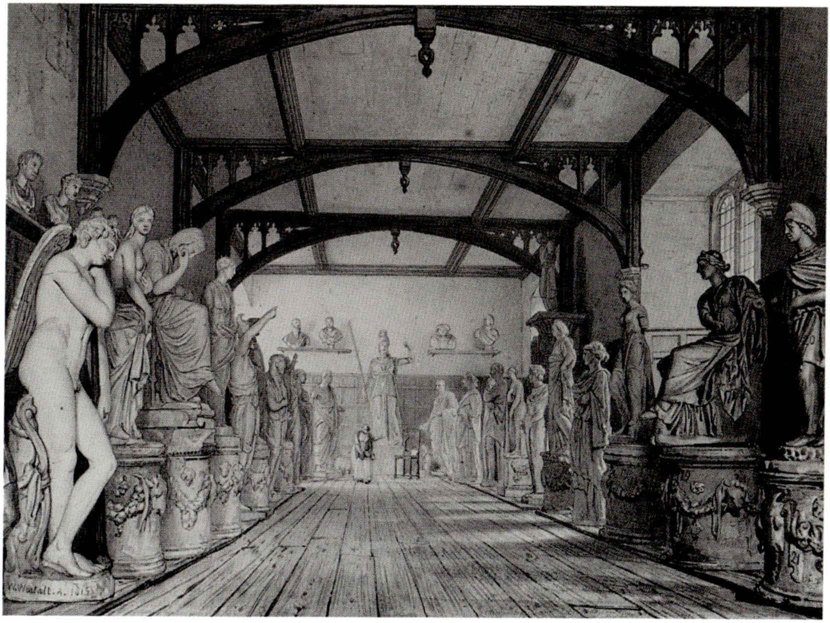

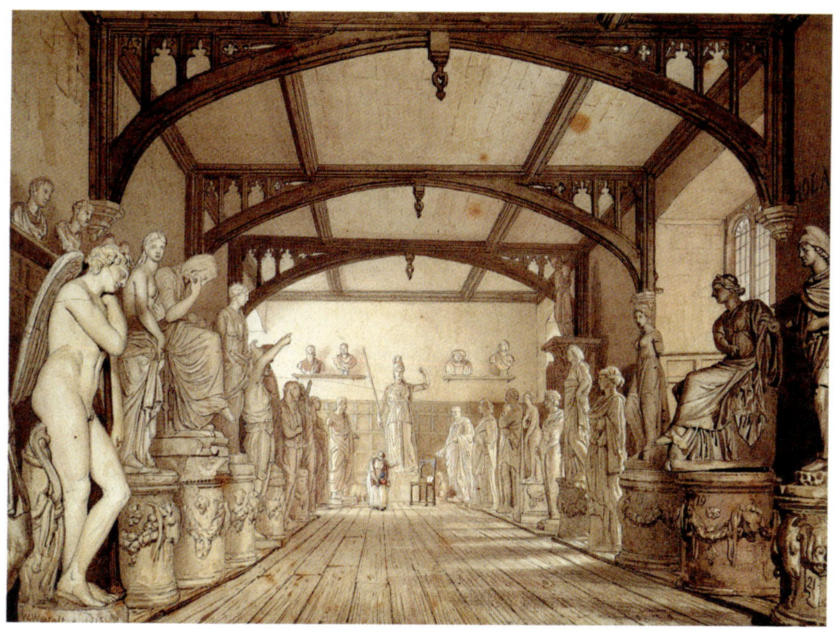

The Oxford Bust

First–third century AD (head); seventeenth century ? (torso)
H.: 66 cm
Pomfret gift 1755 Michaelis 59

The head of this piece is a Roman copy of Pheidias' gold and ivory statue of Aphrodite Urania at Elis, but the torso with one breast bare was perhaps made when the statue was first created in the seventeenth century.

The bust is first recorded in an etching of 1645 by Wenceslaus Hollar (see p. 33) as being in Arundel House and it is identified as 'the empress Faustina, wife of Marcus Aurelius'. It was part of the garden ornament at Easton Neston centred on the 'Tomb of Germanicus' before coming to Oxford in 1755 (see pp. 44–45). It next came to notice in the 1850s when the painter G.F. Watts and Sir Charles Newton found in the Ashmolean 'a beautiful head severed at the neck, and unhappily without the nose. The missing parts were searched for, and they were successful in finding the bust and shoulders'. Watts 'ranked this bust with the best art of Greece in the time of Pheidias... casts were made from the bust and one of these always stood in his studio. The reverence in which this was held by him was so great that it inspired him to paint the transition of Galatea from marble to life'.

This was the painting *The Wife of Pygmalion* exhibited at the Royal Academy of 1868, and subtitled *A translation from the Greek*. It was admired by Gladstone, William Michael Rosetti and Swinburne (who wrote that 'Her shapeliness and state, her sweet majesty and amorous chastity, recall the supreme Venus of Melos'). Many casts of the bust were made, and were until recently still available from a manufacturer in Paris. These were employed as models by nineteenth century neo-classical artists in England, France and America. Among these was Frederick Sandys, who adjusted the corsage of the Oxford Bust for his *Gentle Spring* (of 1865), now in the Ashmolean (Vickers 1991).

Frederick Sandys (1829–1904), *Gentle Spring*.

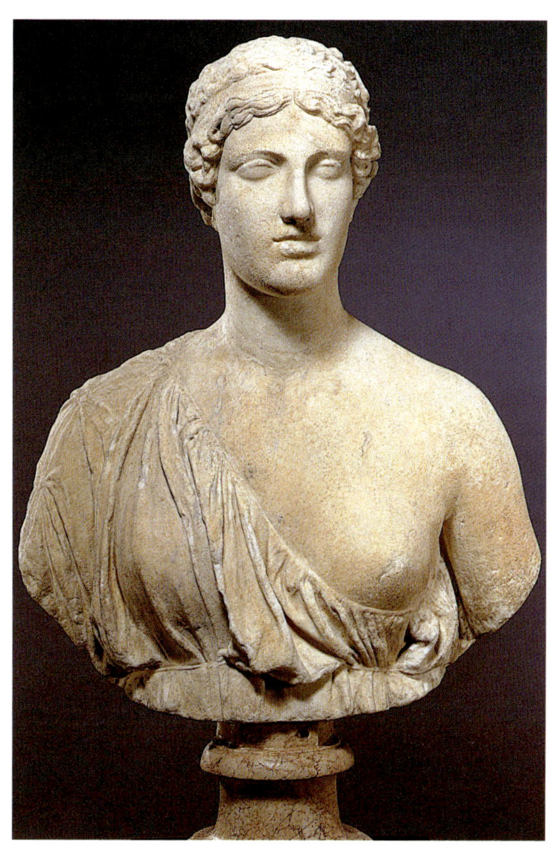

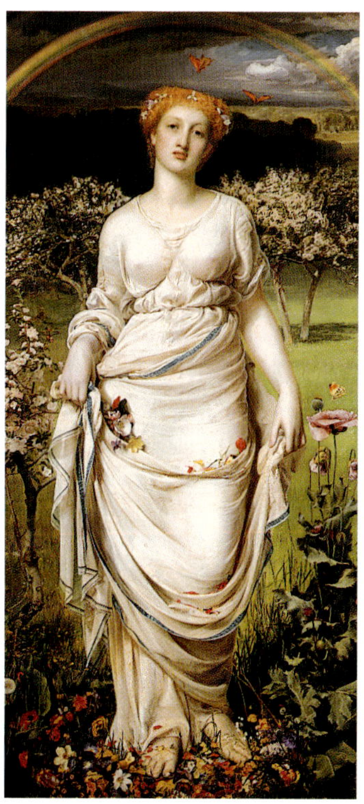

Torso of a Youth

Fifth century BC
H.: 82 cm
Pomfret gift 1755 — Michaelis 52

This forlorn relic is all that is left of what must have been a fine statue in its day; 'its day' being the period during the first half of the fifth century BC when Greek sculptors were able to put archaic rigidity behind them and could achieve more natural poses. The representation of the naked male body was a very popular theme in Greek sculpture. Naked male figures, meant to be portraits, might be erected on the tombs of young men of noble descent. In sanctuaries, similar statues were put up to represent humans, heroes, or gods. At shrines such as Olympia, statues of victorious athletes were common. This statue is made from island marble, probably Parian, and is thought to have been made in a Delian workshop (Kostoglou-Despini 1979). The torso figured among the supporting cast of the 'Tomb of Germanicus' at Easton Neston (see pp. 44–45), being, in the view of George Vertue, 'well executed; so as to be worthy a sculptor's study' (1758, 56).

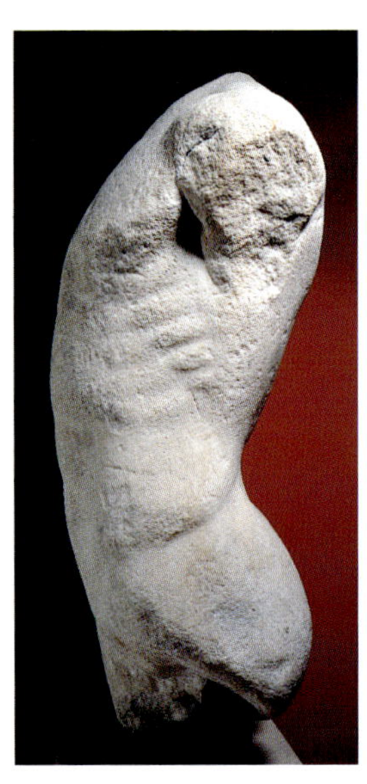

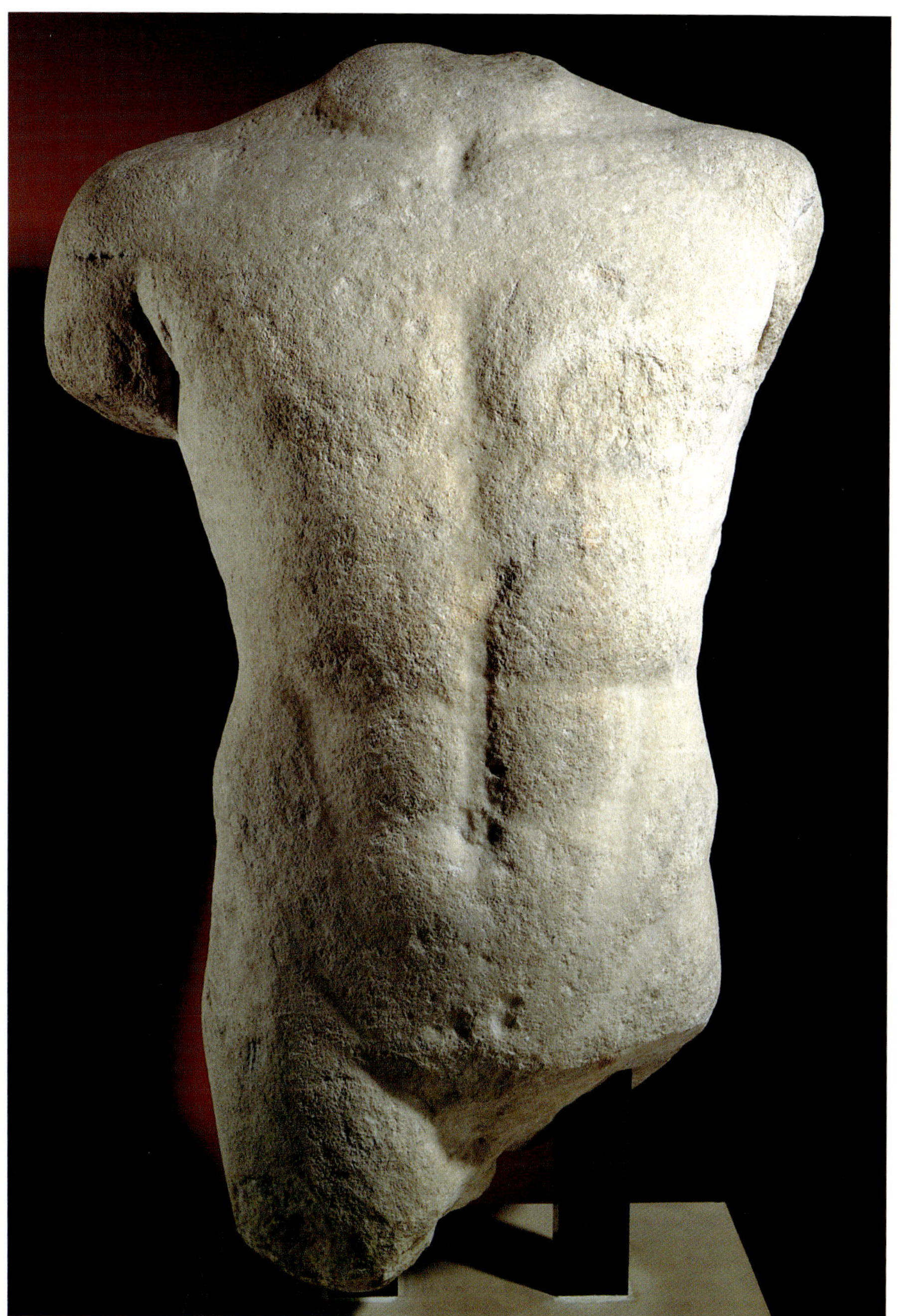

The Metrological Relief

Fifth century BC
H.: 62 cm; extant length: 1.73 m
Pomfret gift 1755 Michaelis 83

The piece is fragmentary and lacks the right end. It shows in relief the upper part of a man with his arms outstretched. Over the complete arm, in low relief, is the outline of a foot, and on the underside of the same arm a deliberately cut cavity representing a fist measurement (Ben-Menahem and Hecht 1985). The relief is clearly concerned with measurement, and there have been many attempts at interpreting its meaning, redoubled in recent years since the discovery of an apparently related relief on the island of Salamis (Dekoulakou-Sideris 1990; Morrison 1991; Berger et al. 1992; Wilson Jones 2000; Wesenberg 2001). The pedimental shape has led some to suppose that the relief served a primarily decorative function in the gable of the porch of a public weights and measures office (e.g. Fernie 1981). And yet, the dimensions described are of considerable interest, and what were once dismissed as puzzling discrepancies can now be seen to belong to different classification values, or variants belong to a logical, elegant and integrated system based on divisions of the Earth's surface at different points on the longitudinal meridian. Thus, for example, the foot in relief measures 29.42 cms, while the proportional foot of the four cubit measurement represented by the outstretched arms is 34.33 cms, a 7 to 6 ratio with the shorter foot (Neal 2000, 238–9).

The Metrological Relief figures large in the arrangements at the 'Tomb of Germanicus' at Easton Neston (see pp. 44–45) and is prominently placed in the allegorical scene showing the 'arrival' of the Arundel/Pomfret marbles in Oxford (see pp. 52–53).

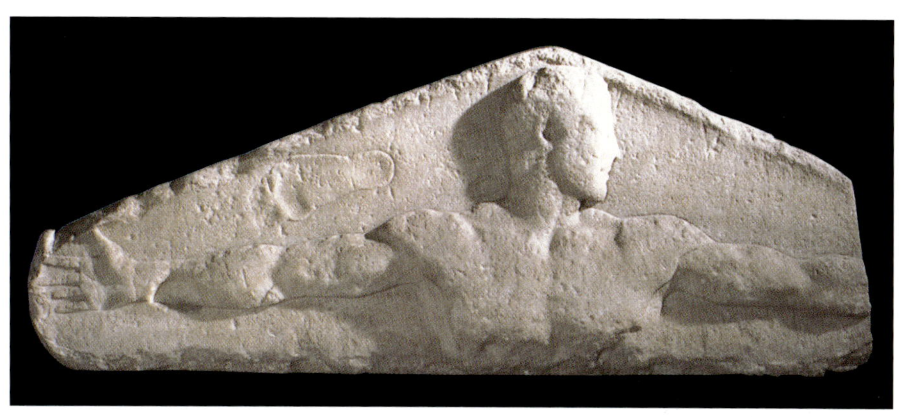

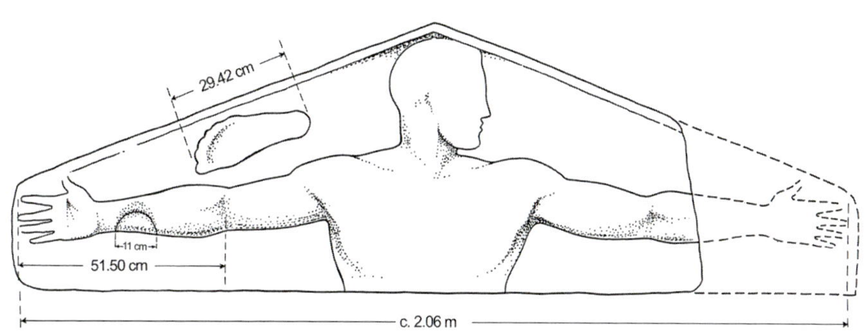
29.42 cm
11 cm
51.50 cm
c. 2.06 m

Athenian Altar

Fifth century BC
H.: 48 cm
Bought with the aid of grants from the Friends of the Ashmolean, Lord McAlpine of West Green, the Art Fund, the Central Purchasing Fund, France Fund and the National Memorial Heritage Fund. AN 1991.294

In 1691 the Duke of Norfolk, grandson of the Earl of Arundel, gave this altar fragment, along with other sculptures, to a family retainer named Boyder or Boydell Cuper. He in turn transferred these sculptures to a pleasure ground he had opened in Lambeth. In 1719 Richard Rawlinson noted that by the Thames Embankment there lay 'a very pleasant garden, in which are fine Walks, well kept in good Order, known by the name of CUPIDS GARDENS. They are the estate of *Jesus College* in *Oxford*, and rented by one who keeps a Publick House; which, with the Conveniency of its Arbours, Walks and several Remains of *Greek* and *Roman* Antiquity, have made this place much frequented'.

This account appears in John Aubrey's posthumously printed *Natural History and Antiquities of Surrey*, where the writer explains that he had been informed that 'the mangled Statues &c. were Part of the Collection brought from *Italy* by the famous Earl of Arundel; but being imperfect, and very much injured by Time, they were not thought valuable enough for a Present to the University of *Oxford*... and much less were they worthy to appear among the beautiful Statues of Lord *Lempster* at *Easton* in *Northamptonshire*; they were therefore, when *Arundell* House was turned into a Street, removed hither, where they received very ill Usage from the Ignorance and Stupidity of those who knew not their Value and are still exposed to the open Air, and Folly of Passers by' (Aubrey 1719 [where (5.pls 1–8), 27 statues and fragments are illustrated; this altar appears on pl. 1]).

Soon afterwards, the remaining 'mangled Statues' were bought by John Freeman of Fawley Court near Henley-on-Thames and Edmund Waller of Hall Barn, Beaconsfield, and having divided the collection between them, they used the sculpture to adorn their country seats. The Ashmolean acquired a fine late fifth-century BC Athenian altar in Pentelic marble from Fawley Court, carved in low relief with the underworld deities Hermes (with a Laconian hound at his feet), Demeter and Persephone (Meunier-Klein 1988).

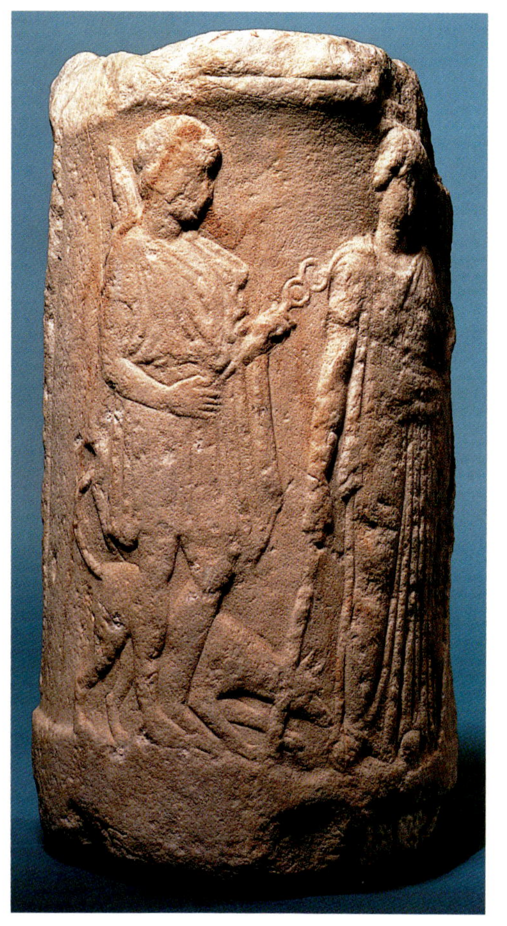

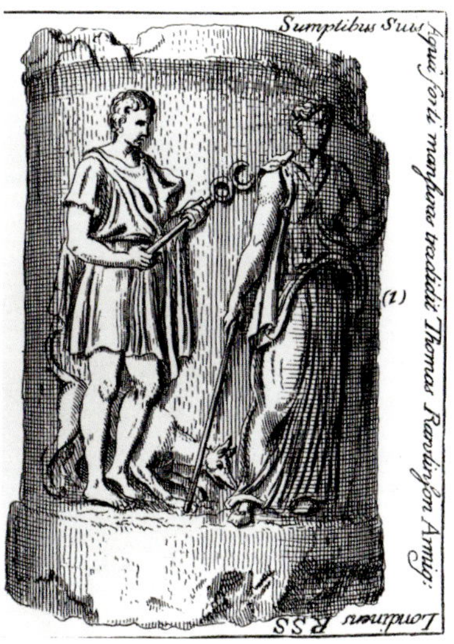

Engraving of the Athenian Altar from J. Aubrey, *The Natural History and Antiquities of the County of Surrey* 5 (1719).

The Arundel Homerus

Third-first century BC
H.: 1.27 m
Bought with the aid of the Friends of the Ashmolean, the Victoria and Albert Museum Purchase Grant Fund, the Art Fund, the Littauer Fund, the Ashmolean Bomford Bequest Fund and the Central Purchasing Fund.
AN 1984.45

Among the statues illustrated in Aubrey 1719 and taken by John Freeman to Fawley Court was a large marble statue of a man standing with his hands joined across his chest (5. pl. 5). Until the 1960s this stood outside as a garden ornament, but was subsequently on loan to the Ashmolean, and eventually acquired by the Museum.

This statue had once played a supporting role in the history of European painting. Rubens saw it in Italy and later used his sketch as the basis for Chronos in the background of Louvre's *Le Gouvernement de la Reine* of 1622–1625. Meanwhile, the statue had entered the Arundel collection, where it can be seen in Mytens's portrait of the Earl (see p. 17). The statue had come to be known as 'Homerus', on the basis of George Cedrenus's description of a statue of Homer at Constantinople having 'the hands clasped under the chest' (Haynes 1974; Vickers 1992, 247–8), but the identification is unlikely. It probably formed part of a portrait statue of an individual who lived in the later Hellenistic period.

Peter Paul Rubens, *Homerus*.
Küpferstichkabinett, Staatliche Museen zu Berlin.

Peter Paul Rubens,
Le Gouvernment de la Reine,
Paris, Musée du Louvre.

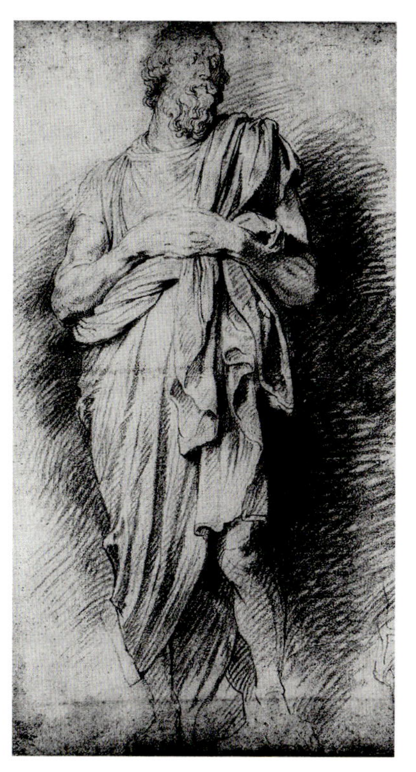

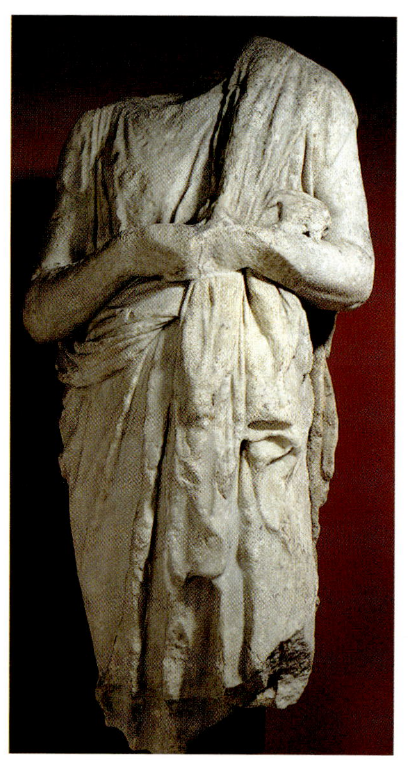

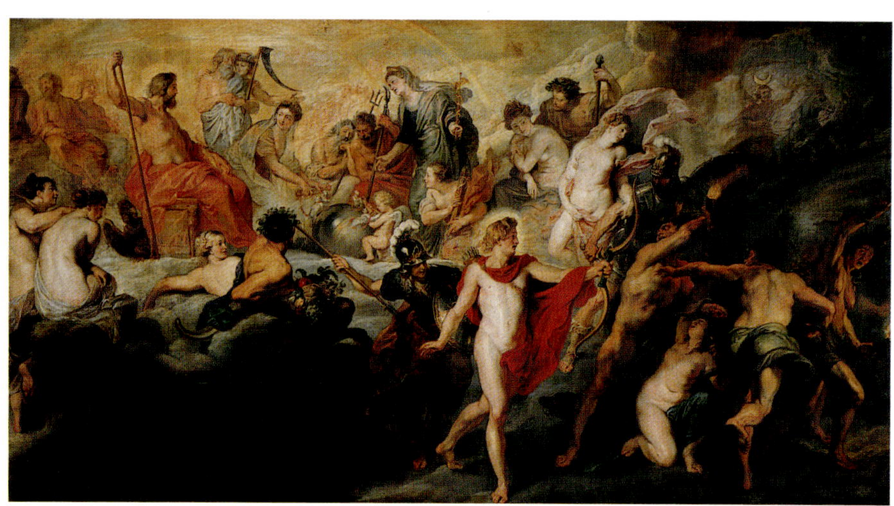

Wounded Amazon

First century BC–third century AD
H.: 1.04 m
Pomfret gift 1755 Michaelis 24

There are many extant Roman marble copies of at least three types of Greek fifth-century bronze Wounded Amazon statues (l–r below: the Amazon Sciarra, the Amazon Sosicles, the Amazon Mattei; Weber 1977). This piece corresponds to the one on the left. Pliny, the Roman encyclopaedist, tells the story of a competition for a statue of an Amazon for the temple of Artemis at Ephesus. The artists involved (who included Pheidias, Polycleitus, and Cresilas) had to choose the winner, and this proved to be the Amazon 'which each artist had placed second to his own', namely the one made by Polycleitus (*HN* 34.53). The Ashmolean's Amazon may well relate to such a project, and the suggestion has been made that it is a copy of Polycleitus's entry. She wears a flimsy chiton, belted at the waist. The wound is visible beneath the right armpit.

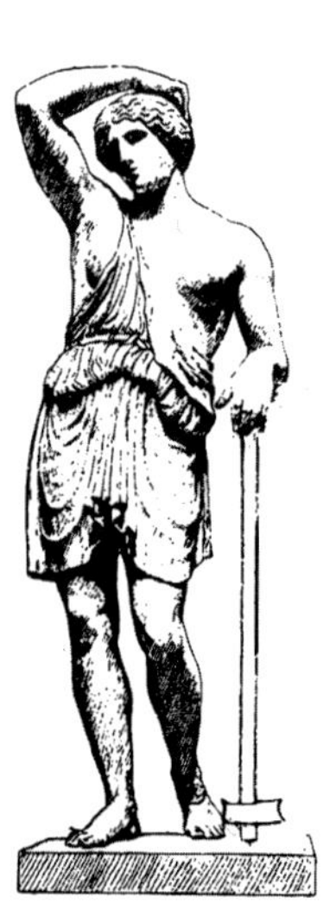

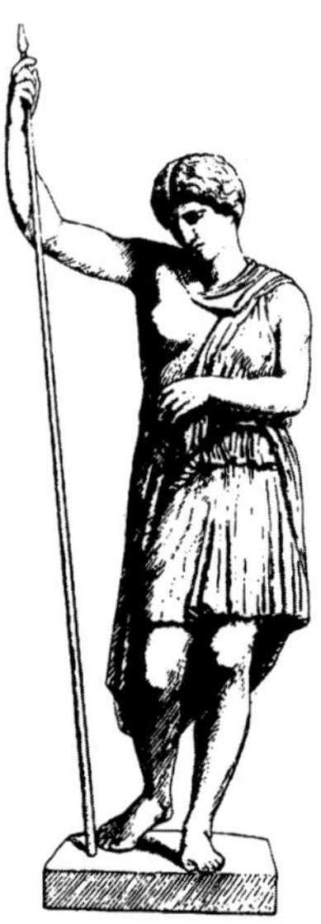

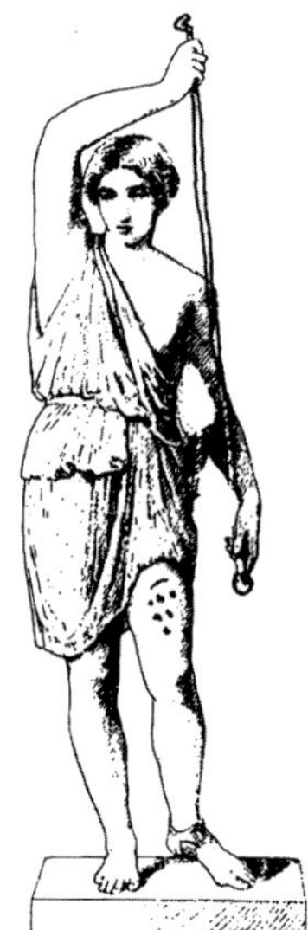

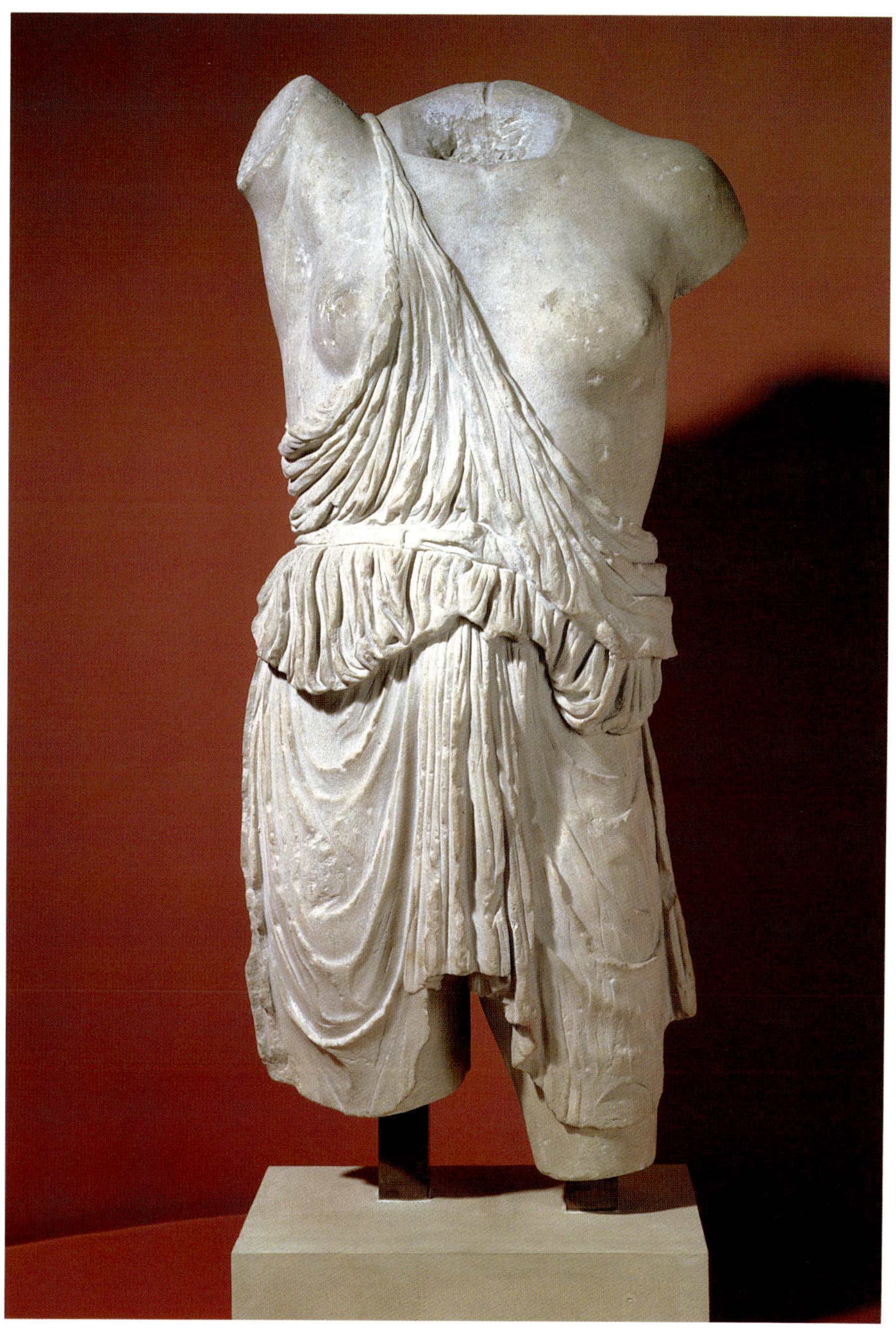

Menander

First–third century AD
H.: 50 cm
Pomfret gift 1755 Michaelis 66

The ivy wreath suggests that this bust is the portrait of a writer. It was once identified as 'Pindar the poet' by George Vertue (1758, 59). There are more than fifty Roman period versions copies of a lost Greek original that was later tentatively identified as the playwright Menander (Richter 1965, 2.232, no. 26). This identification was confirmed when a small bronze bust in the J. Paul Getty Museum was seen to be inscribed in Greek with the name *Menandros*, and taken to be a faithful copy of a statue of Menander in the Theatre of Dionysus at Athens by Cephisodotus and Timarchus, the sons of Praxiteles, in the fourth century BC (Ashmole 1973).

Menander (342/1–293/2 BC), who was 'cross-eyed but of nimble mind' (Suda), was the inventor of situation comedy. He wrote more than 100 plays during a career that lasted about thirty-three years. His characters spoke in the language of contemporary Athens and were concerned not with traditional myths, but with everyday life. Boy meets girl, anxious parents, unwanted pregnancies, long-lost relatives were the themes of his plays. They were extraordinarily popular in antiquity and were adapted by the Roman playwrights, Plautus and Terence. Only one, his *Dyskolos* ('the Peevish Man'), has survived complete.

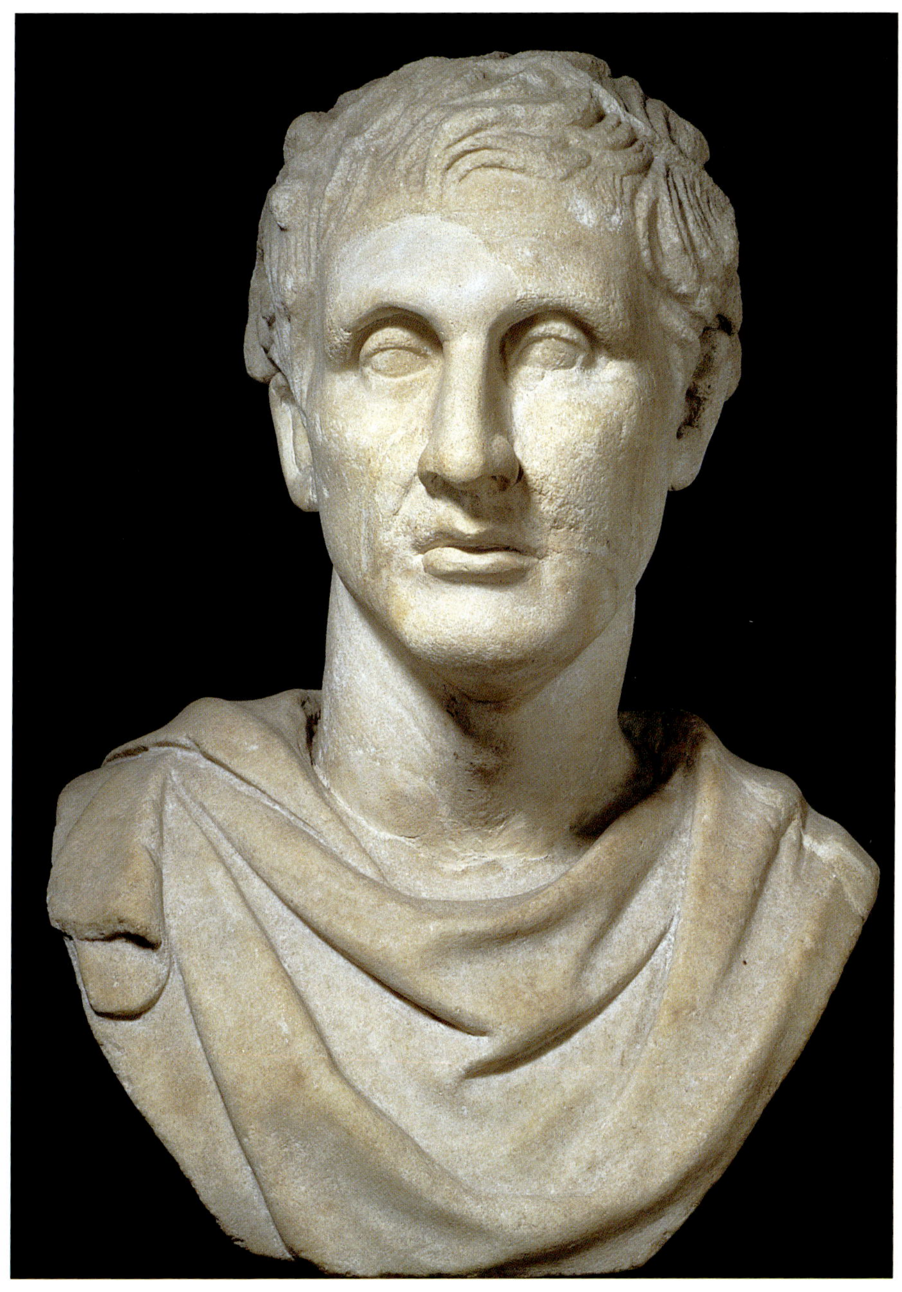

The Snagge Head

Fourth–first century BC
H.: 33 cm
Anonymous gift 1918 AN G. 1199

The following anecdote is told by Sir Mountstewart Grant Duff in his diary:

> Judge Snagge said to me this afternoon: 'I bought recently one of the Arundel marbles for a sovereign'.
>
> 'How did that happen?' I enquired.
>
> 'I saw', he said 'a navvy at a station on the Underground Railway with a head in his hand. At the first glance I thought it was an ordinary plaster cast, but on looking closer I saw that it was of marble, and asked the man where he had got it.'
>
> 'I got it', he replied, 'in digging the foundations of a house in Surrey Street'.
>
> 'What do you mean to do with it?' I asked
>
> 'I mean to sell it, I want a sovereign for it'.
>
> 'I will be happy to give you a sovereign,' I rejoined, 'if you will show me where you got it.'
>
> 'This the man proceeded to do, and the foreman confirmed his story, adding that he was allowed to take away any rubbish he might find. I gave him the sovereign, jumped into a hansom, and went straight to the British Museum, where it was identified as a fine Greek head of an athlete in Parian marble' (Grant Duff 1930, 133).

The head was presented to the Ashmolean in 1918.

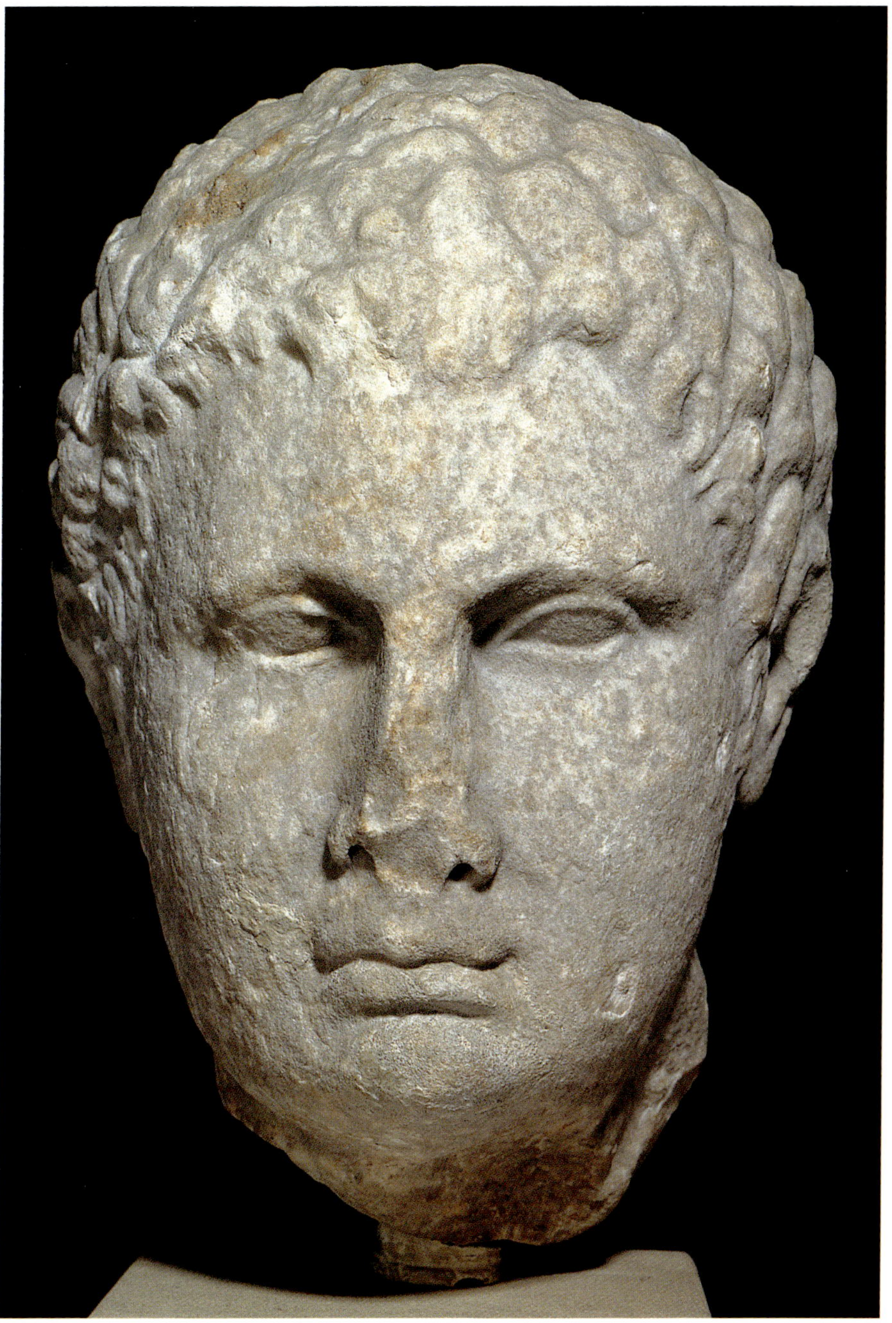

Hellenistic Statue of a Woman

Second–first century BC
H.: 2.03 m
Pomfret gift — Michaelis 5

This over-lifesize statue is now a ruin, but when new will have had inset in the socket at the neck the recognisable features of an individual Greek matron. The pose is characteristic: the weight resting on the right leg, and the left leg somewhat advanced. The cloak (*himation*) covers the right arm (the left one is a later reconstruction), and the folds of the dress (the *chiton*) can be seen beneath it. The left foot was also added later. A similar statue can be seen today standing in a house on Delos, and given that the Greek islands were the hunting grounds of William Petty, Arundel's agent, it perhaps hints at a likely source for our piece.

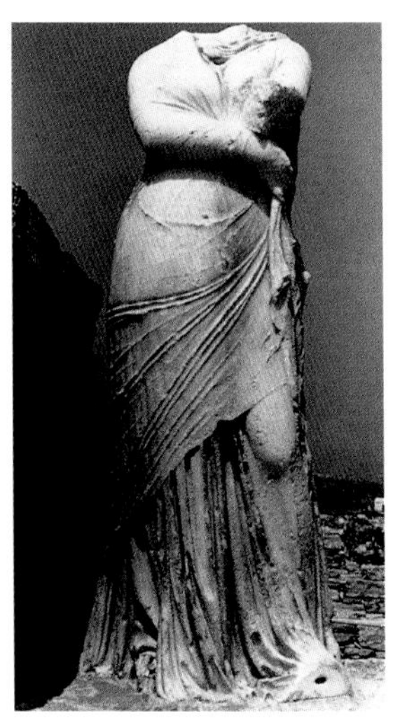

Above: Statue of a Woman on Delos

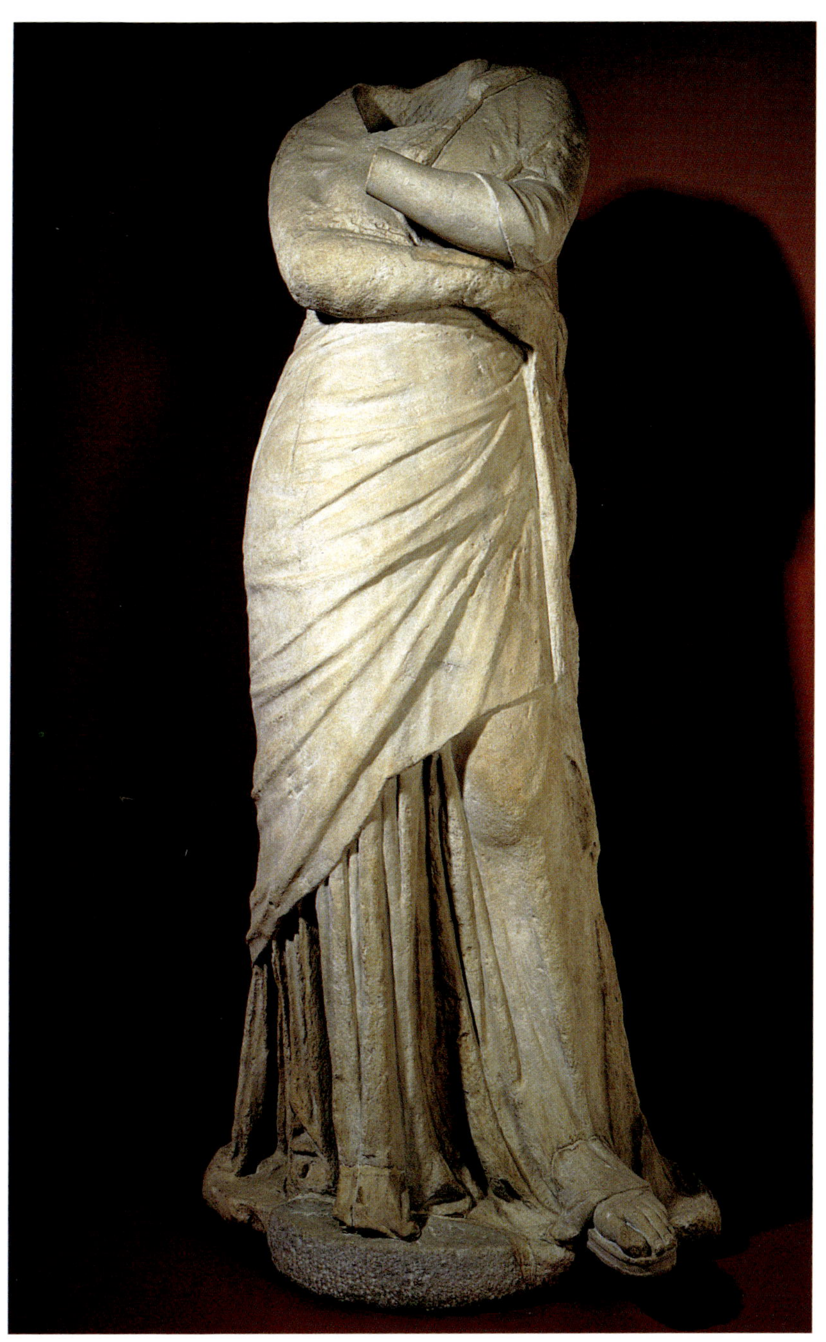

Students' Victory

Second half of the first century AD
H.: 67 cm; W.: 78 cm
Howard gift 1667 Michaelis 135

This relief commemorates a victory at Eleusis, won by a group of students (*epheboi*) at an Athenian gymnasium, by the assistant director, the *sophronistes* Athenaios. The scene of Heracles resting under a tree, on his famous lion-skin, with his quiver and club near him is highly appropriate. Heracles was considered to be a mythological founder and patron of gymnasia. His endurance, physical strength and his Labours made him a role model for young men in ancient Greece. This votive relief is carved from Pentelic marble and dates from the second half of the first century AD. Like most other ancient sculpture, the relief would originally have been brightly painted.

Engraving of the Students' Victory inscription from H. Prideaux, *Marmora Oxoniensia* (1676), p. 83.

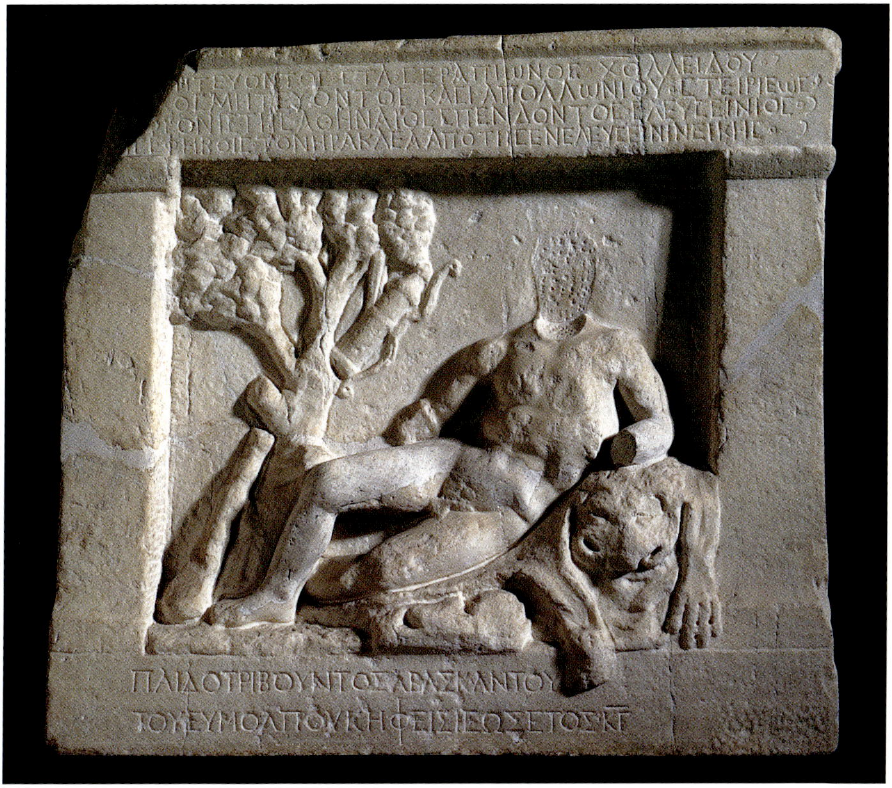

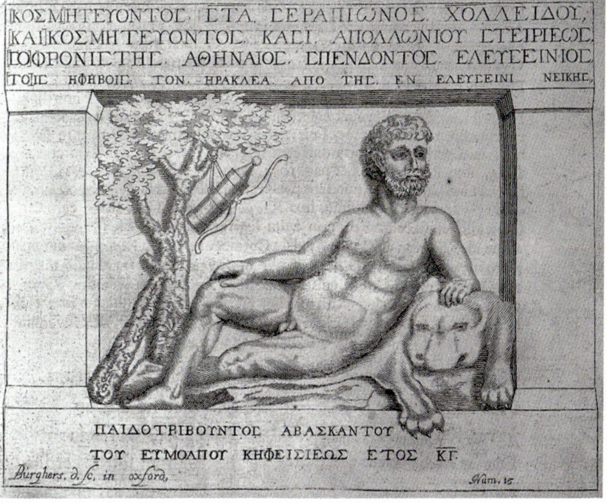
[ΚΟΣΜ]ΗΤΕΥΟΝΤΟΣ ΕΤΑ ΣΕΡΑΠΙΩΝΟΣ ΧΟΛΛΕΙΔΟΥ,
[ΚΑΙ]ΚΟΣΜΗΤΕΥΟΝΤΟΣ ΚΑΣΙ ΑΠΟΛΛΩΝΙΟΥ ΣΤΕΙΡΙΕΩΣ
[ΣΩ]ΦΡΟΝΙΣΤΗΣ ΑΘΗΝΑΙΟΣ ΣΠΕΝΔΟΝΤΟΣ ΕΛΕΥΣΕΙΝΙΟΣ
[ΤΟ]ΙΣ ΗΦΗΒΟΙΣ ΤΟΝ ΗΡΑΚΛΕΑ ΑΠΟ ΤΗΣ ΕΝ ΕΛΕΥΣΕΙΝΙ ΝΕΙΚΗΣ,
ΠΑΙΔΟΤΡΙΒΟΥΝΤΟΣ ΑΒΑΣΚΑΝΤΟΥ
ΤΟΥ ΕΥΜΟΛΠΟΥ ΚΗΦΕΙΣΙΕΩΣ ΕΤΟΣ ΚΓ
Burghers. d. sc. in oxford,
Num. 15

Athena

First–third century AD
H. 2.70 m
Pomfret gift 1755 Michaelis 19

Athena was the goddess born of Zeus in a rather curious fashion. Zeus had swallowed the pregnant Metis, but then developed headaches. These were cured by a blow from the axe of Hephaestus, when Athena sprang fully armed from her father's head. This statue is a Roman-period version of a well known type whose origins lie in the fifth century BC. The most magnificent Athena was that made from gold and ivory by Pheidias for the Parthenon on the Acropolis at Athens, a statue which stood more than eleven metres high (Lapatin 2001). Our piece is of more modest proportions, though still colossal. Only the torso is original, and over the breast can be seen one of Athena's attributes: the aegis with its snaky fringe and head of the gorgon Medusa, with which enemies could be held at bay. The head is an eighteenth century restoration, probably by Guelfi (see p. 47), and the raised left arm is probably authentic, and thus departs from known parallels. The girdled *chiton* with its overfold, however, recalls that of Pheidias's chryselephantine Athena Parthenos.

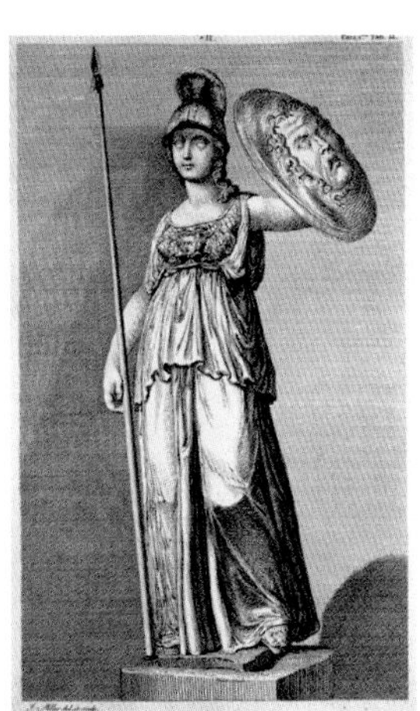

Engraving of Athena from R. Chandler, *Marmora Oxoniensia* (1763).

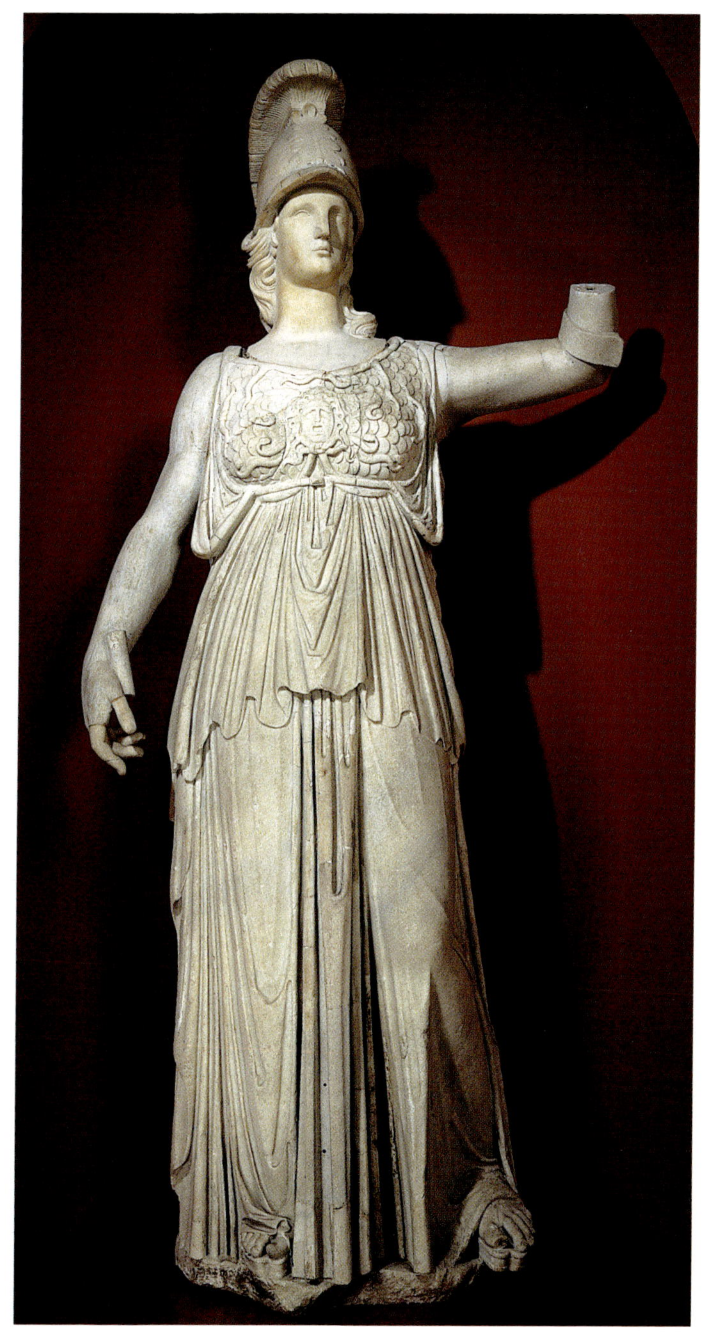

Me, Claudius?

First century AD
H.: 34 cm
Pomfret gift 1755 Michaelis 69

This battered over-lifesize portrait head has served over the years as something of an academic football, having been variously identified as Augustus (Gardner), Agrippa (Michaelis 1882, 557), Britannicus (Jucker 1982, 268, n. 95), and Claudius. This is not so extraordinary since as portraits of members of the Julio-Claudian family are often superficially similar. The weight of scholarly opinion has recently come down in favour of Claudius (emperor AD 41–54), and it is generally agreed that our piece belongs to a group now known as the 'Cassel type' (Poulsen 1962, 65; Fittschen 1977, 51, n. 22; Queyrel 1986, 287–8, n. 2; Salzmann 1990, 170, 173). It may even be that our head is a reworked portrait of Caligula, Claudius's less than illustrious predecessor whose memory underwent condemnation (*damnatio memoriae*) after his death in AD 41 (Goette 1984, 727).

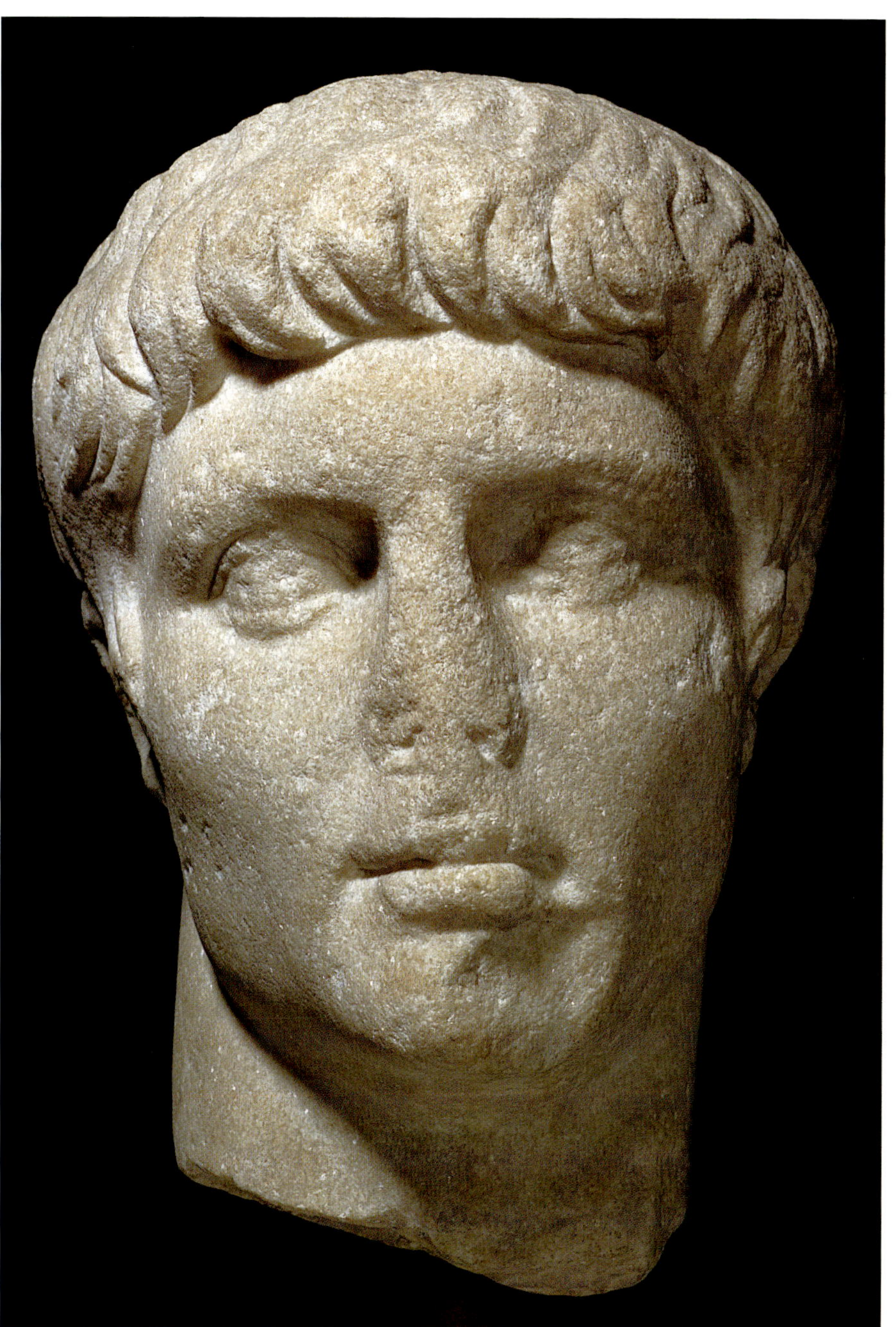

Doctor and Wife

First century AD
83 x 89 cm
Howard gift 1667

Michaelis 155;
Chandler 1763, 2.72

The tombstone of the doctor Claudius Agathemerus and his grim-faced wife Myrtale originally came from Rome and is said to have been acquired from 'the sculptor Chr. Status', who lived near the church of S. Andrea delle Fratte. The inscription reads, 'Here lie I, Claudius Agathemerus, a doctor widely known as a swift healer of disease; this monument brings together with me my consort Myrtale; we are with the blessed in Elysium'. The busts are placed side by side and show the doctor as a beardless man wearing a toga; his wife is represented as an older lady wearing a high curled wig, characteristic of the second half of the first century AD. Our Claudius Agathemerus is otherwise known as the friend and fellow-pupil of the poet Persius.

Engraving of the Doctor and Wife from H. Prideaux, *Marmora Oxoniensia* (1676), p. 77.

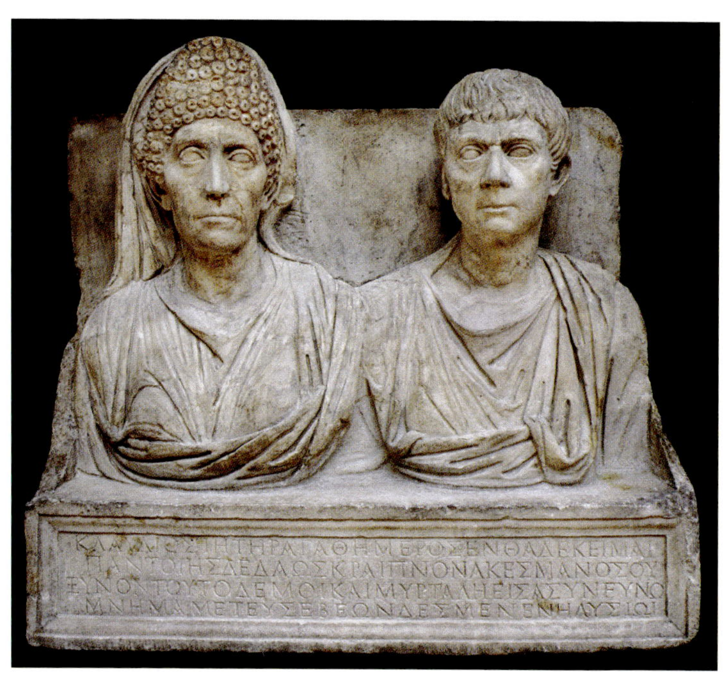

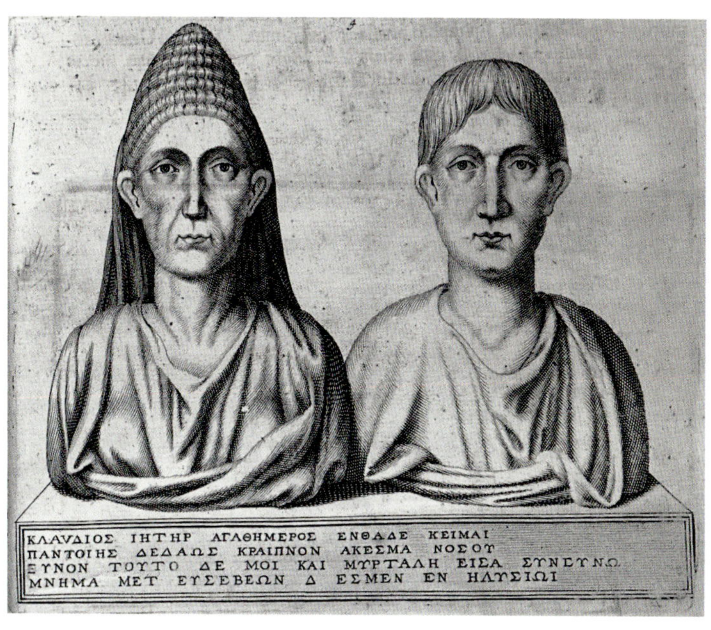
ΚΛΑΥΔΙΟΣ ΙΗΤΗΡ ΑΓΑΘΗΜΕΡΟΣ ΕΝΘΑΔΕ ΚΕΙΜΑΙ
ΠΑΝΤΟΙΗΣ ΔΕΔΑΩΣ ΚΡΑΙΠΝΟΝ ΑΚΕΣΜΑ ΝΟΣΟΥ
ΞΥΝΟΝ ΤΟΥΤΟ ΔΕ ΜΟΙ ΚΑΙ ΜΥΡΤΑΛΗ ΕΙΣΑ ΣΥΝΕΥΝΩ
ΜΝΗΜΑ ΜΕΤ ΕΥΣΕΒΕΩΝ Δ ΕΣΜΕΝ ΕΝ ΗΛΥΣΙΩΙ

Arundel Marbles elsewhere

Not all the Arundel Marbles came to Oxford, as we have seen. There may be pieces still buried in and around the site of Arundel House, and others have been discovered over the years in contexts with some kind of Arundel connection. A fragment of the Great Altar of Zeus at Pergamon, taken in the eighteenth century to Worksop, was on the point of being broken up for chips to place on graves in 1963 when it was acquired by the Worksop Public Library (Haynes 1963). Another fragment of a giant (known to Rubens [Vickers 1981]) found its way to Fawley Court, Henley, where it was placed in a roundel on the façade of a Gothick ruin (Haynes, 1972; 1975, 16–17). It is now in a private collection in London.

In 1677, Henry Howard, Duke of Norfolk, sold a large number marble busts to Thomas Herbert, later eighth Earl of Pembroke, who used them to adorn Wilton House near Salisbury. It is, however, impossible to say which of the many busts there came from the Arundel collection. Some of the residue of the Marbles in London found their way to Kennington, and some were given in the eighteenth century to Lord Burlington; a late Hellenistic funerary relief can still be seen built into the base of an obelisk in the grounds of Chiswick House (Haynes 1968, 210). At Hall Barn, Beaconsfield, there survive a draped female statue and an Asklepios (Haynes 1972, fig. 16). There is now documentary evidence that five statues once at Thorpe Hall (Bailey 1996, 112) once belonged to the Arundel collection (information from Nick Davey). There are seven Greek altars, a votive foot, and two Dieussart portraits at Arundel Castle in Sussex.

The most important absentee, however, is the granite obelisk from the Circus of Maxentius once known as 'Mr Petty's Needle' that was acquired in Rome on Arundel's behalf (Howarth 1985, 136–8). The English Civil War prevented its removal to London, and it is now the crowning glory of Bernini's *Fountain of the Four Rivers* in Piazza Navona (1648–51), built on the site of the Stadium of Domitian in Rome (Iversen 1968, 76–92).

Clockwise: Worksop Giant; Fawley Court Giant; Bernini Fountain, Rome; Hall Barn, Asklepios; Chiswick house relief

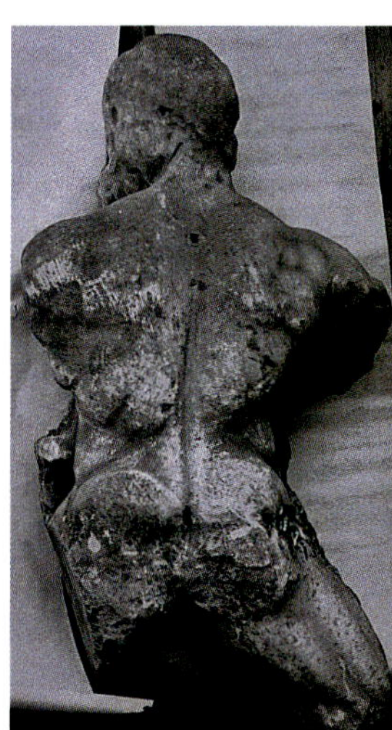

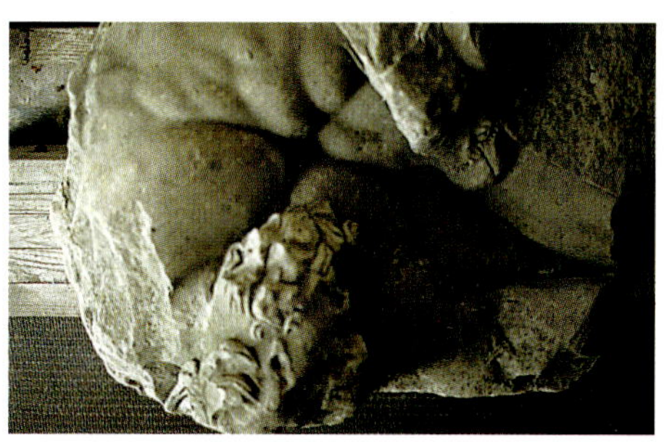

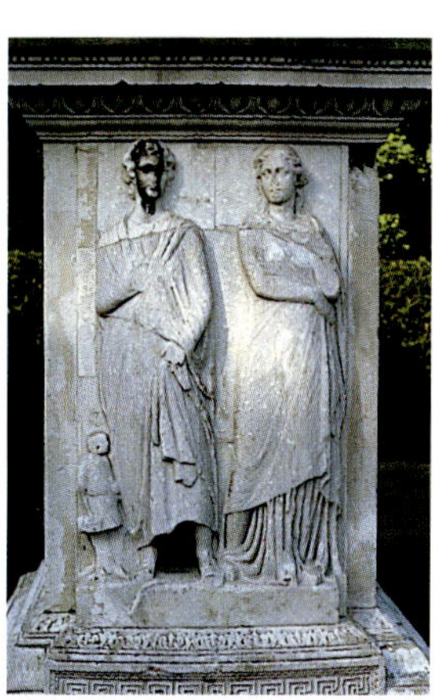

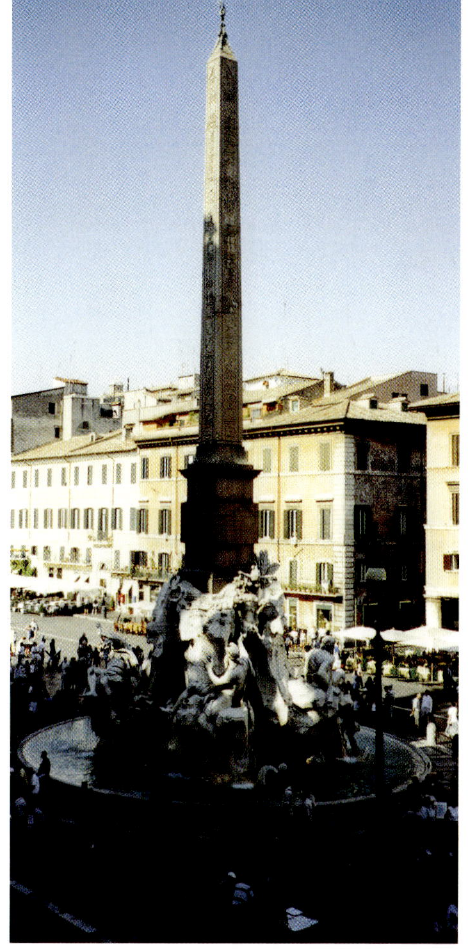

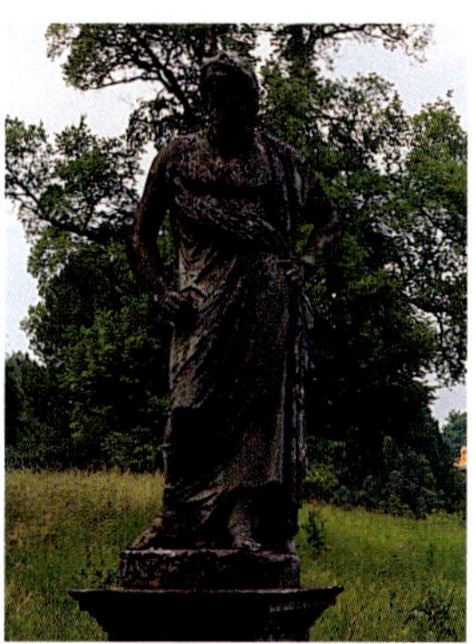

Bibliography

Amelung, W. (1903–56), *Die Sculpturen des Vatikanischen Museums: im Auftrage und unter Mitwirkung des Kaiserlich Deutschen Archäologischen Instituts (Römischen Abteilung)* (Berlin).

Ackermann, R. (1814), *History of the University of Oxford, its colleges, halls, and public buildings* (London).

Angelicoussis, E. (2004), 'The collection of classical sculptures of the Earl of Arundel, 'Father of vertue in England'', *Journal of the History of Collections*, 16: 143–59.

Ashmole, B. (1973), 'Menander: an inscribed bust', *American Journal of Archaeology* 77: 61.

Aubrey, J. (1719), *The Natural History and Antiquities of the County of Surrey* 5 (London).

Bailey, B.A. (1996). *Northamptonshire in the Early Eighteenth Century: the drawings of Peter Tillemans and others* (Northampton).

Ben-Menahem, H. and N.S. Hecht, N.S. (1985), 'A modest addendum to 'The Greek metrological relief in Oxford'', *Antiquaries Journal* 65: 139–40.

Berger, E., B. Müller-Huber, B. and L. Thommen, L. (1992), *Der Entwurf des Künstlers, Bilhauerkanon in der Antike und Neuzeit* (Basel).

Birch, T. (1848), *The Court and Times of James the First illustrated by authentic and confidential letters, from various public and private collections* (London).

Boehringer, R. and E. (1939), *Homer* (Breslau).

Chandler, R. (1763), *Marmora Oxoniensia* (Oxford).

Clarendon, E., Earl of Hyde (1888), *History of the Rebellion and Civil Wars in England* (London).

Clark, A. (1895), *The Life and Times of Anthony Wood, Antiquary, of Oxford, 1632–1695, described by himself*, vol. 4: Addenda (Oxford).

Colvin, H. (1994), 'The Pomfret portrait', *The Ashmolean* 26: 6–7.

Cook, B.F. (1974), 'The classical marbles from the Arundel House site', *Transactions of the London and Middlesex Archaeological Society*, 26: 247–51, pls 7–10.

Dallaway, J. (1800), *Anecdotes of the Arts in England; or, Comparative remarks on architecture, sculpture, and painting, chiefly illustr. by specimens at Oxford* (London).

Dekoulakou-Sideris, I. (1990), 'A metrological relief from Salamis', *American Journal of Archaeology* 94: 445–51.

Dunn Macray, W. (1888), *The history of the Rebellion and Civil Wars in England Begun in the Year 1641* (Oxford).

Edwards, E. (1870), *Lives of the Founders of the British Museum* (London).

Evelyn, *Diary* = E.S. de Beer (ed.), *The Diary of John Evelyn* (Oxford, 1952).

Fernie, E. (1981), 'The Greek metrological relief in Oxford', *Antiquaries Journal* 61: 256–63.

Fittschen, K. (1977), *Katalog der antiken Skulpturen in Schloss Erbach* (*Archäologische Forschungen* 3) (Berlin).

Fletcher, J. (1996), 'The Arundels in the Veneto', *Apollo* 144: 63–9.

Gardner, P. Manuscript notes on Michaelis 1882 in the Department of Antiquities' records.

Giometti, C. (1999), 'Giovanni Battista Guelfi: new discoveries', *The Sculpture Journal* 3: 26–43.

Giometti, C. (2000), 'Gentlemen of Virtue. Morality and representation in English eighteenth-century tomb sculpture', in C. Sicca and A. Yarrington, *The Lustrous Trade* (Leicester).

Godfrey, R. (1996), 'Hollar's prints for the Earl of Arundel', *Apollo* 144: 36–8.

Goette, H. (1984), 'Antike Skulpturen im Herzog Anton-Ulrich-Museum Braunschweig', *Archäologischer Anzeiger*, 711–44.

Grant Duff, M.E. (1930), *A Victorian Vintage; being a selection of the best stories from the diaries of the Right Hon. Sir Mountstuart E. Grant Duff*, ed. A.T. Bassett (London).

Harding, R. (1996), 'John Evelyn, Hendrick van der Borcht the Younger and Wenceslaus Hollar', *Apollo* 144: 39–44.

Haynes, D.E.L. (1963), 'The Worksop relief', *Jahrbuch der Berliner Museen* 5: 5–13.

Haynes, D.E.L. (1968), 'The Arundel Marbles: the formation and dispersal of the first great collection of classical sculpture in England', *Archaeology* 21: 85–91, 206–11.

Haynes, D.E.L. (1972a), 'Alte Funde neu entdeckt', *Archäologischer Anzeiger*: 731–42.

Haynes, D.E.L. (1972b), 'The Fawley Court relief', *Apollo* 96: 6–11.

Haynes, D.E.L. (1974), 'The Arundel "Homerus" rediscovered', *The J. Paul Getty Museum Journal* 1: 73–9.

Haynes, D.E.L. (1975), *The Arundel Marbles* (Oxford).

Hervey, M.F.S. (1921), *The Life, Correspondence and Collections of Thomas Howard, Earl of Arundel, 'Father of Vertu in England'* (London).

Hess, J. (1950), 'Lord Arundel in Rom und sein Auftrag an den Bildhauer Egidio Moretti', *English Miscellany* 1: 197–219.

Houfe, S. (1977), 'A taste for the

Gothick: diaries of the Countess of Pomfret 1', *Country Life*, March 24: 728–30; 'Antiquarian inclinations; diaries of the Countess of Pomfret 2', *ibid.*, March 31: 800–2.

Howard, C. (1769), *Historical Anecdotes of Some of the Howard Family* (London).

Howarth, D. (1985), *Lord Arundel and his Circle* (London).

Iversen, E. (1968), Obelisks in *Exile* 1: *The Obelisks of Rome* (Copenhagen).

Jacoby, J. (1929) *Die Fragmente der griechischen Historiker* 2B (Leiden).

Jaffé, D. et al. (1996), 'The Earl and Countess of Arundel: Renaissance collectors', *Apollo* August: 1–37.

Jucker, H. (1981), 'Iulisch-Claudische Kaiser-und Prinzenporträts als "Palimpseste",' *Jahrbuch des Deutschen Archäologischen Instituts* 96: 236–316.

Junius, F. (1637), *De pictura veterum* (Amsterdam).

Junius, F. (1638), *The Painting of the Ancients: 'De pictura veterum' according to the English translation* (London).

Junius, F. (1991), *Franciscus Junius: the Literature of Classical Art* (ed. K. Aldrich, P. Fehl, and R. Fehl) (Berkeley).

Kostoglou-Despini, A. (1979), *Problems of Parian Sculpture in the 5th Century BC* (Thessaloniki).

Lapatin, K. (2001), *Chryselephantine Statuary in the Ancient Mediterranean World* (Oxford).

Lapierre, A. (2004), *Le voleur d'éternité: la vie aventureuse de William Petty, érudite, esthète et brigand* (Paris).

Lloyd, D. (1677), *Memoires of the lives ... of those... personages that suffered... for the Protestant religion and... allegiance to their soveraigne... from... 1637 to... 1666* (London).

Mansuelli, G. (1958) *Galleria degli Uffizi, Le Sculture* (Florence).

Meulen, M. van der (1975), *Petrus Paulus Rubens Antiquarius: Collector and Copyist of Antique Gems* (Alphen aan den Rijn).

Meunier-Klein, M. (1988), 'Quelques autels à décor figuré sculpté et les problèmes qu'ils posent: identification du monument en tant qu' autel. Interprétation de l'iconographie, proposition de datation', in *Bulletin de liaison de la Société des Amis de la Bibliothèque Salomon Reinach* n.s. 6: 39–56, figs 1–6.

Michaelis, A. (1882), *Ancient Marbles in Great Britain* (Cambridge).

Morrison, J. (1991), 'Ancient Greek measures of length in nautical contexts', *Antiquity* 65: 298–305.

Mytton, T. (1758), *A poem on the Pomfret statues* (Oxford).

Neal, J. (2000), *All Done with Mirrors* (London).

Patterson, F. (1931–38), 'Essays from the Columbia manuscript perhaps by John Milton: Of Statues and Antiquities', *The Works of John Milton* 18: 258–61 (New York).

Peacham, H. (1634), *The Compleat Gentleman*, 2nd edn (London).

Penny, N. (1992), *Catalogue of European Sculpture in the Ashmolean Museum* (Oxford).

Penny, N. and Howarth, D. (1985), *Thomas Howard, Earl of Arundel : patronage and collecting in the seventeenth century* (Oxford).

Petter, H.M. 1974. *The Oxford Almanacks* (Oxford).

Poulsen, V. (1962), *Les portraits romains* 1 (Copenhagen).

Prideaux, H. (1676), *Marmora Oxoniensia ex Arundellianis, Seldenianis alliisque conflata* (Oxford).

Queyrel, F. (1986), 'Les sculptures', in R. Étienne et J.-P. Braun, *Ténos I : le sanctuaire de Poséidon et d'Amphitrite* (Bibliothèque des écoles françaises d'Athènes et de Rome 263) (Paris), 267–320.

Richter, G.M.A. (1965), *The Portraits of the Greeks* (London).

Robert, C. (1890), *Antiken Sarkophag-Reliefs* 2: Mythologische Cyclen (Berlin).

Salzmann, D. (1990), Antike Porträts im *Römisch-Germanischen Museum Köln. Wissenschaftliche Kataloge des RGM*, 5 (= *Kölner Jahrbuch für Vor- und Frühgeschichte*) 23: 131–220.

Scarisbrick, D. (1996), 'The Arundel gem cabinet', *Apollo* 144: 45–8.

Scott, J. (2003), *The Pleasures of Antiquity: British collectors of Greece and Rome* (London).

Selden, J. (1628) *Marmora Arundeliana* (London).

Sharpe, K. (1978), 'The earl of Arundel, his circle and the opposition to the duke of Buckingham, 1618–1628', *Faction and parliament*, ed. K. Sharpe (1978), 1–42.

Stukeley, W. (1724), *Itinerarium curiosum; or, An account of the antiquitys and remarkable curiositys in nature or art, observ'd in travels thro' Great Brittan* (London).

Sturdy, D. and N. Moorcraft, N. (1999), 'Christopher Wren and Oxford's Garden of Antiquities,' *Minerva* 10: 25–28.

Tenison, T. (1679), *Baconiana* (London).

Uhlig, L. (ed.) (1982). *Johann Joachim Winckelmann: Gedanken über die Nachahmung der griechischen Werke in der Malerei und Bildhauerkunst. Sendschreiben. Erläuterung* (Stuttgart).

Vertue, G. (1758), *A Description of Easton-Neston in Northamptonshire, the Seat of the*

Right Honourable the Earl of Pomfret; with an Account of the curious antique Statues, Busto's, Urns, &c. In B. Fairfax, *A Catalogue of the Curious Collection of Pictures of George Villiers, Duke of Buckingham* (London).

Vertue, G. (1934), 'Vertue Note Books, volume III', *Walpole Society* 22: 1–162.

Vickers, M. (1978), 'Rupert of the Rhine, a new portrait by Dieussart and Bernini's Charles I', *Apollo* 97: 161–169.

Vickers, M. (1979a), 'Lord Arundel's Roman patronage: two 'lost' statues by Egidio Moretti rediscovered,' *Apollo* 98: 224–225.

Vickers, M. (1979b), 'Hollar and the Arundel Marbles', *Städel Jahrbuch* n.s. 7: 126–132.

Vickers, M. (1980), 'The changing face of Henry VIII,' *Country Life*, April 24: 1248–1249.

Vickers, M. (1981), 'A new source for Rubens' "Descent from the Cross" in Antwerp', *Pantheon* 39: 140.2

Vickers, M. (1985), 'The Felix Gem,' in Penny and Howarth 1985: 73–4.
Vickers, M. (1988–89), 'Germanicus' Tomb', *The Ashmolean* 15: 6–8.

Vickers, M. (1991), 'The "Oxford Bust"', *The Ashmolean* 20: 6–8.

Vickers, M. (1992), 'Acquisitions of Greek and Etruscan antiquities by the Ashmolean Museum, Oxford 1981–90', *Journal of Hellenic Studies* 112: 246–8, pls 7–8.

Vickers, M. (1997), 'Two vast and trunkless legs of stone', *The Ashmolean* 32: 13.

Vickers, M. (forthcoming), '"A pillar of ye Temple of Apollo at Delphos" and Winckelmann's columns from Delos in English gardens', *Beiträge der Winckelmann-Gesellschaft.*

Walker, E. (1705), *Historical Discourses, upon several occasions* (London).

Walters, H.B. (1899), *Catalogue of the bronzes, Greek, Roman, and Etruscan, in the Department of Greek and Roman Antiquities, British Museum* (London).

Webb, M. I. (1995), 'Giovanni Battista Guelfi', *Burlington Magazine* 97: 139–45, 260.

Weber, M. (1977), 'Die Amazonen von Ephesos', *Jahrbuch des Deutschen Archäologischen Instituts* 91: 28–96.

Wesenberg, B. (2001), 'Vitruv und Leonardo in Salamis: "Vitruvs Proportionsfigur" und die metrologischen Reliefs', *Jahrbuch des Deutschen Archäologischen Instituts* 116: 357–80.

White, C. (1995), *Anthony van Dyck*: Thomas Howard the Earl of Arundel (Malibu, Calif.).

Wilson Jones, M. (2000), 'Doric measure and architectural design 1: the evidence of the relief from Salamis', *American Journal of Archaeology* 104: 73–93.

Appendix

There is in the Department of Antiquities at the Ashmolean a copy of an anonymous poem entitled *On the Pomfret Statues,* to which the name of the author Thomas Mytton has been added in manuscript. It was published for Daniel Prince in Oxford in 1758. It carries a somewhat melancholy 'Advertisement' that reads as follows: 'The Verses on the Statues were to have been spoken in the Theatre, at *Oxford*, at the Commemoration which the Countess of POMFRET honour'd with her Presence'; poor Mr Mytton clearly did not have the opportunity of reciting his poem on the great day. We reproduce it here.

On the Pomfret statues

When Science first, forlorn, forsaken Maid !

By tyrants frighted, from *Italia* stray'd :

Chearless and weary long she wing'd her flight

O'er the black realms of Ignorance, and Night ;

'Till thro' the gloom, she sees a streaming ray

Gild the white tops of *Albion's* cliffs with day :

For Freedom, here inthron'd, with lib'ral hand,

Show'r'd down her blessings on the fav'rite land ;

And from the golden crown, the grac'd her head,

A mild and genial lustre round her spread.

Here, as on hov'ring wing, she, pois'd, surveys
The verdant fields, and azure-circling seas,
Lo ! *Oxford's* flow'ry plains attract her eyes ;
Thither, with joyful speed the Goddess flies :
Here, wand'ring charm'd, to Isis' flood she came,
And bath'd her, fainty, in the cooling stream.
Here follow soon, the whole *Aonian* quire,
And strike again the long-neglected lyre.
Here Architecture taught her sons to raise
An hundred spiry temples, to her praise.
Here Kings, and Princes seek her aid divine,
And pour their treasures on her ample shrine.

And see ! advancing thro' the splendid train,
Where Bounty leads her POMFRET to the fane.
And see ! — all hail ! — a rev'rend marble band,
In awful state, approach, at her command :
Gods, to whom *Romans* oft have bent the knee ;
Statues, which, form'd while *Greece* and *Rome* were free,
Bear down the steep of time, the Patriot's face ;
The Sage's calm, or Heroes rougher grace ;

Brows, with eternal bays, and laurels crown'd ;
Lips, whence persuasion's hony stream'd around ;
Limbs never gall'd by slav'ry's iron chain ;
Breasts, where old Honour held her constant reign.
The sculptur'd column, and the breathing bust,
Stand here, deliver'd from oblivion's dust.

But pause — approach, with reverential fear,
The stone that frowns with *Tully's* face severe :
Stern as when arm'd in Freedom's cause he shone,
When Vice and *Catiline* assail'd her throne.
Oppress'd with gen'rous grief, he view'd her woe ;
He view'd, and rush'd indignant on the foe.
Her vengeful thunder Eloquence supplies ;
Guilt hears it burst appall'd, and blasted Faction dies.
So when in ancient bard's romantic lays,
Thro' desert wilds a palfrey'd damsel strays,
Now flies some dragon fierce, or Painim's flame ;
Now tow'rs inchanted hold the hapless dame.
At length, dispatch'd by Heaven, for virtue's aid,
Some val'rous knight with fairy-temper'd blade,
Destroys the monsters, and sets free the maid.

Here oft in *Marius's* look, the eye shall trace
Those lines majestic, and that awful grace,
At which the fell assassin, stuck with dread,
Dropp'd from his trembling arm the sword, and fled.

But who is she ? the thoughtful head reclin'd,
And pensive mein, denote a musing mind.
Queen of the sigh profound, and trickling cheek,
These marks the sage *Melpomene* bespeak ;
Who oft delights, in ev'ning's dusky ray,
In shape of some lone traveller, to stray
Where, prone in ruin, lies imperial *Rome* ;
Or thus, beneath some temple's mould'ring dome,
To sit: while, sad, she weeps the waste of Age,
Sees Kings, and Heroes fall beneath his rage :
O'er prostrate Sculpture views the tyrant stride
Insulting all the pomp of human pride.
Spurn'd by his foot, while prone along the ground
Arcs, obeliscs, and vases tumble 'round ;
Stretch'd in the dust, sees mighty Empire lie ;
And Grandeur glide, an empty phantom, by.

Then o'er the land she sheds a silent tear,
Once to each Science, to each Grace so dear ;
Thro' whose gay-smiling plains, in days of yore,
In nectar'd streams, Truth pour'd her sacred lore :
Where, nurs'd, and chear'd by Freedom's genial ray,
Bloom'd ev'ry Art, and flourish'd ev'ry Bay :
Where *Tiber* often, as he roll'd along,
Has stopt, inraptur'd with the Muses song :
There now, the tyrant's rage since Freedom fled,
Each with'ring art reclines it's languid head :
The Muses sooth old *Tiber's* ear no more,
They drop their lyres, and ravag'd seats deplore :
Ign'rance, and Superstition haunt the shade,
Where once the Sage, and Wisdom, musing, stray'd :
No more the brave, or patriot thought can warm,
Fear chills each breast, and slackens ev'ry arm.

But hence awhile, sad Goddess ! nor profane
With tear, or heaving sigh this festal scene.
See ! raptur'd *Clio* sweeps th' enliv'ning strings,
While warring Chiefs, and Valor's praise she sings.

Be this thy strain, when *Gallia's* haughty lord,
For treaties broke, shall feel th' avenging sword.
But gentler virtues now thy praises claim ;
Be *Isis*' Friend and Patroness thy theme :
Let Bounty's praise the grateful verse prolong,
And POMFRET'S name inspire the flowing Song.